DUNG BAG ROAD

DUNG

A Personal Account

BAG

of Depression

ROAD

and Recovery

SABRINA BECK, BS

MANY**SEASONS**PRESS

2022 • Mesa, Arizona

FIRST EDITION

Dung Bag Road
A Personal Account of Depression and Recovery

Copyright © 2022 by SaBrina Beck, BS

Published by Many Seasons Press
An imprint of Multimedia Publishing Project
PO Box 50553
Mesa, Arizona 85208-0028
480-939-9689 | MultimediaPublishingProject.com

Cover & book interior designed by Yolie Hernandez
(AZBookDesigner@icloud.com)

Paperback ISBN: 978-1-956203-02-8
e-Book ISBN: 978-1-956203-06-6

Library of Congress Control Number: 2022941798

Printed in the United States of America.

Dedication

THIS BOOK IS DEDICATED to my husband, Rob, and my three daughters, Vanessa, Victoria, and Graciela, for their unconditional love and forgiveness for all that I did not know or realize about being a wife and mother. The path to my recovery was paved largely in part because of your support. You are my people for life.

To my mother, for being an example of resilience, kindness, and success despite challenges that were beyond your control. You are my parent, my guide, and my forever friend.

I would also like to dedicate this book to the therapists who were in the right place at the right time to help me crawl, walk, and move in the direction of developing a foundation for better mental health.

Contents

Acknowledgments

MY HUSBAND, ROB, AND MY DAUGHTERS, Vanessa, Victoria, and Graciela, gave me their support and encouragement in my quest to write this book. Also, my mom and ex-mother-in-law, Johnnie. They understood it had to do with my past experiences and traumas from my perspective and my time spent in outpatient therapy. They have all seen a difference in my growth and development since completing CBT and investing in individual counseling sessions. It was a difficult time for our family and could have ended more broken than it began. To each of you, thank you for allowing me the time and space to heal my inner child and for the grace of connection.

Retired Health Educator Cindy Davis and lifelong friends Lisa Houg and Sylvia Coughlin were kind enough to read my early manuscript and provide feedback that helped keep my emotions in check, lending credibility to the book's overall theme. Ladies, you are my soul sisters, and I would be lost in the friendship department without you.

My husband was my sounding board when I needed to decompress after going through the most challenging chapters. He was there to comfort me with open arms. Rob listened to me verbally process some of the events as more details surfaced with each manuscript review.

There were many heroes along the way who shared their kindness and humanity with my girls and me. Karen, Beth, Deanna, many Lisas, Robin, Kim, Bonita, Patty, Jodi, Denese, Joan, ZZ Sisters, Erica, Lynn, Helise, David and Annette, the Dorcas Quilters, and many more heroes who shined their light on me. Thank you from the deepest place in my heart.

Lastly, my mother, my sister, Gigi, and my BFF, Lisa, I would not have made it this far without you.

Preface

$\mathcal{J}$ WAS 25 YEARS OLD WHEN I RAN AWAY FROM HOME. In June of 1991, I boarded a flight in my hometown of Phoenix, Arizona. My destination was Seoul, South Korea. By 1994, I had moved back to the United States, landing in Metropolis, Illinois, after living in Valdosta, Georgia. One year later, I petitioned the court to dissolve my marriage and allow me to move back to Arizona with my two little girls. The petition to divorce succeeded but no relocation. A subsequent petition also resulted in a denial. It felt like a dead end. There was no other choice but to find a path of survival.

I am now 56 years old and have made many trips to and from the place I will always call home, and the home where for many of those years away, I felt imprisoned. After time, opportunities, and hard work, I have finally reached a peaceful destination.

Included in that path of survival are another marriage and another daughter, which makes three on both counts. Thankfully, my husband loves Arizona and my family as much as I do. In planning for our future, we have purchased a home there. Our grandkids have named it the "vacation house," and our home in Illinois is the "lake house."

It was the dry heat of the summertime in 2021, and we were once again visiting family and friends. We've got the visiting seasons all wrong, I know. I love that dry. Catching up with lifelong friends and family also fills my cup. This particular visit truly felt like a vacation. In the past several years, there have been times when my return was in response to an emergent situation to help take care of our mother or brother. This visit was oddly peaceful.

I came with my husband and brother. While my husband starts his online workday and my brother sleeps, I walk, sometimes two miles and up to five miles. I've got to get up extra early to get my walk in and return home in time to wake up my brother. We have a routine to follow each morning. I see many rabbits and lizards during my walks, and a coyote crossed my path on one occasion! I stopped dead in my tracks. It was about 30 feet in front of me. Deep breath, a reactive U-Turn, and I left as calmly as possible.

There are many paths to walk, run, bike, hike, or travel in any direction my mind and feet could take me. I see others on the trail and folks in cars on their way to work. The desert scenery brings me a kind of peace that I cannot find elsewhere. Someday, I will return home for good. I got lost a few times and needed to use my GPS to get back to our neighborhood. Thank goodness for helpful tools.

One day, when I returned from my walk, I was ready to open "my blue folder" that I had brought. I've held onto it for 13 years. Its contents are memories of living in a very dark place. I tried looking at it from time to time but would quickly shove it back on a shelf until the next time. I wasn't ready to face what had happened to me. Not what was wrong with me, but what happened to me. This time was "the next time," and I was ready to dive into its contents.

My blue folder contains drawings I made when I attended an outpatient cognitive behavioral therapy program back in 2008. Some of them are doodles, and some include depictions of emotions that had been haunting me for decades. I drew when I couldn't speak the words to describe my inner thoughts and feelings, most of which carried tons of pain, shame, guilt, and denial. The drawings portray personal traumas that had been deeply embedded in my psyche and left to become worse and interfere with my adult life. The birthdays kept coming, but the emotional development stalled. My poor inner-child was making it up as she went along. There was no exit until a mental bridge collapsed and caused an emotional pile-up. I was liable and needed to do the work to recover.

Now, I will walk down a different road that may give readers insight into how traumas, physical or emotional— perceived or real— can negatively impact your life and the people around you. My traumas were left unaddressed. As a result, the events from adverse childhood experiences (girl-child), two marriages and two divorces (woman-girl), and a third marriage (broken-woman) had a significant impact on my mental health. These events impacted my view of the world and the people in it. To face the drawings in my blue folder meant I was in a healthy and healed place. Reflecting on the recovery process, I am grateful to be on a different road—one of living life and enjoying the beautiful scenery.

I am no longer a therapy patient, nor do I require medication. As a lifelong learner, I continue to process, practice and add to what I learned. I have discovered along the way a wonderful, imperfect, beautiful woman. I am also amazed by the people I call my family and friends; they are a blessing. Walking as a functional but traumatized human being was exhausting and put me on the brink of collapse. Today, I can walk with a lighter load and better understand my mental health with good fortune and hard work.

I held on to that blue folder for a reason. Only now do I realize why. The stories I share are specific and do not contain the many good life experiences that kept me moving forward, and there are many. They include the ones that had the most impact and were a guidepost in how I coped with the worthless experiences that made a home in my dung bag.

Documenting my struggles and how I overcome them was not an easy task, but it sure was healing. It was a full-on dump of my dung bag. Perhaps some unwanted visitors have made a home in your dung bag. If it is empty, count yourself blessed. If not, I hope my story helps prompt and promote a path to healing. I hope you, too, can love yourself where you are and build a foundation for better mental health.

I am not a licensed counselor or clinical therapist and cannot give you any advice from that perspective. My story doesn't intend to replace professional treatment and care; instead, to show one person's account of depression and recovery. Cognitive-behavioral therapy worked for me, but the cure to my depression took more than one treatment practice. I've been practicing ever since. It's hard, but it's worth it. And so are you!

Introduction

"*I* WANT MY KIDS BACK! I want my kids back! Oh, gosh, I can't do this anymore! You take Graciela and let the other girls go with their dad. You can have everything. I'll go back home and live by myself, far away from them where I can't hurt them or you. I lost them, I lost them; I can't believe I lost them."

These are the cries of a frantic mother who just lost her job and believed that she lost her two teen daughters in the same night. She was in a crisis because of the perceived possible loss of her daughters, not her job. They didn't want anything to do with her anymore. Their mother had moved out of their home into a new house and wanted to divorce their stepdad for no apparent reasons or any they could understand. She had abandoned them, and now they wanted nothing to do with her.

The girls' mother, Sabrina, had done her best to take care of her two oldest daughters after a tumultuous divorce. She would do everything to protect them, even with a broken spirit. They were teenagers now and had experienced the over-protective patterns their mother exercised throughout the years. They saw her tired, angry, sad, lonely, loving, and caring. She was always home for them and took care of them, but she went too far when she got a job and moved out.

When her crisis occurred, she had been remarried for nine years and had another child, a seven-year-old daughter. Sabrina told her husband to take care of their little girl, but he wouldn't let her give up on them and life so easily. He stayed with her when others were telling him to let her go. Together they came up with a plan to get help processing what had happened that evening and why she felt so defeated. They didn't know that the help she needed and would receive would take her down a dark and dirty road, starting with her childhood, adolescence, young adult years, and two divorces. That dirty road she would take is the Dung Bag Road.

PART I

Girl-Child

PART I RECALLS EXPERIENCES during my formative and adolescence years. They recount specific events that influenced my views of family.

HAVING BEEN RAISED BY MY MOTHER WAS A BLESSING. Her kind soul has been a constant reminder of how I should treat people. Her parenting skills could have been better, but they also could have been worse. The same goes for other adults in my life.

WHAT MATTERS IS THAT I AM ALIVE AND WELL.

Where Did She Go?

Having a parent with a history of depression
is a known risk factor for depression in
children and teens. (Boyles, 2005).

AFTER SCHOOL

ONE DAY, I CAME HOME FROM SCHOOL to find Frank asleep and sprawled out on the couch in his boxers. One of his arms was outstretched towards the floor where a liquor bottle, a gun, and an ammo box lay close by. I was in the third grade and should have been learning division. Instead, I would learn about what could happen when a person has too much to drink.

Frank was my brother's dad and was married to my mother. My mom, stepdad, two older sisters, my little brother, and I lived in an apartment together. Frank had been previously married and had three other children older than us. Sometimes they would stay with us. What I remember about Frank, other than the couch scene, was his dinner table commands for us kids to eat our peas before getting up from the table. I wouldn't say I liked the texture and color of peas, so I was still at the table when they turned cold. Until I came up with a plan: I would put them in my mouth, pretend to chew, spit them out in a napkin, then ask to be excused to go to the bathroom. I would then spit them out in the toilet, flush, and return to the table. I was a very clever young child. I am sure he never figured that one out.

After finding him on the couch, I quietly played pick-up sticks on the kitchen floor. *Where is my mom?* The air was still and quiet; no one else was home. I didn't know if that was a good thing. I remember my mom screaming out one time that it was too quiet. This situation was confusing for me.

After a while, the front door slowly opened, and my sister appeared. "Shh, come on," she whispered. She took me by the hand, and we were gone. Frank did not reside with us after that.

TEMPORARY RELOCATION

Our aunt and uncle took only my sister Gigi and me to their house to stay for a while. Since it was in the middle of the school year, we were transferred from Grant to Joseph Zito Elementary, where our cousins attended. For some reason, I remember holding a free lunch pass and feeling very comforted by that. I don't know where my other sister and little brother went. They were as gone as my mother. Where was she, and why did she leave us? Not one adult explained why my mom left to the heart and mind of an eight-year-old child.

Living with my aunt Marie and uncle Danny was interesting. Marie was the boss lady and punished for misbehavior. There were mornings when my teeny tiny bottom met the end of a swinging belt because of bedwetting accidents.

I didn't do it on purpose. One night I dreamt that I walked into the bathroom to pee, only to wake up and find that I had still wet the bed. My girl-child brain could not understand or explain why it was happening. These accidents wouldn't go away for many years. "For most kids, nighttime wetting, also known as nocturnal enuresis, is normal and goes away naturally with time." (*When Will My Child Stop Bedwetting?*, 2021).

Another morning ritual was the brushing and pulling of our long, stringy black hair. Marie would secure our ponytails so tight that our eyes would squish backward towards our ears. Now, that hurt.

Despite the spankings and squishy eyes, we adjusted to our new living arrangements. Soon after, this man showed up. He was there to take us to the hospital to see our mom. That's where she was, at a hospital. This man looked familiar, and our aunt and uncle let us go with him. He was our dad, or at least his name, George, was listed on our birth certificates. We never lived with him, and he never showed up for visitation time with us, but he was there now.

VISITING HOURS

My mom didn't look sick or hurt. I didn't see any bandages, blood, or tubes sticking out of her body. *Why was she in the hospital?* My mom was quiet and sad, so there wasn't much conversation in the cold hospital room. She was just cold, quiet, and sad. She made a yarn-wrapped popsicle stick cross in craft therapy—a souvenir from our visit with her. No one was smiling.

The time went by, and soon we were reunited with our mom. She still seemed sad, but we went on with our lives without Frank. We moved to a new apartment near 12th Street and Northern Avenue, in Phoenix, by my Nana Angela, and transferred to Madison Simis Elementary school, where I finished my third-grade year. We stayed there until the middle of seventh grade.

MY MOM

Much later, I would better understand what my mom endured. That pain she had that needed to be treated by doctors may have been connected to my stepdad's condition when I found him on the couch. I don't know what happened that day I came home from school, but I suspect the couch scene was a factor in my mom's admission to the hospital. She needed to get better before she could come back home to us. Back then, I heard the adults use the term 'nervous breakdown.' Nowadays, a diagnosis can identify depression, anxiety, or other mental health conditions listed in the *Diagnostic and Statistical Manual of Mental Disorders* (DSM-5) (About DSM-5, n.d.).

In the years that followed, I don't remember too many times when my mom would smile or laugh. I would see the "tiredness" and feel the aura of sadness around my mom for many years. She was present but not fully there. 'I love you' was seldom exchanged. The maternal affection was absent and left me to feel disconnected and unimportant throughout my teenage years. *Is that normal?* She even forgot my 16th birthday. *How could she forget?* I suppose I can understand as there is likely an index of birthdays in her mind.

She is the eldest of 13 siblings. Three others may have left this world before leaving the hospital. With ten brothers and two sisters, my mom would say, "It felt like my mom was having a baby every year." When it was my mom's turn to enter motherhood, she did so in a similar fashion... 1963, 1964, and 1965. My brother was born in 1971.

I know very little about my mom's upbringing except that it was crowded with siblings and numerous challenges. The wall to her past was bricked, and very few stories were allowed to seep through the cracks. At the time of writing this book, she is in the process of writing her memoirs. I can't wait to read what it was like for her growing up in a deep-rooted, Hispanic-cultured family. She was born in 1940 and was a teen in the 50s. She told me her dad lived around the corner from where she grew up and remembers walking with her sister to see him. Sadly, paternal affection was absent. Her father died when she was a young girl, and she would live to see two other father figures (stepdads) come and go.

Another story that seeped through was told when my husband, Rob, and I were at her house for one of our visits. Without prompting, she began to talk about her first husband, Louie. We sat and listened compassionately and carefully. I could see this was a therapeutic moment for her, and certainly, it was knowledge previously unknown to me. The marriage to Louie ended with an interesting twist and turn. As my husband and I drove away, I shared how rare it was for my mom to be so open. Opening up was not her modus operandi. I was a teenager when I learned that she and George never married. This meant her maternal experience started as a single mother with a single income and multiple heartbreaks and challenges. Later she would marry Frank, my little brother's dad, and still shares his surname to match my brother's. The last name given to me at birth means '*nada*,' and has resentment, not pride, attached to it.

My mom was a busy woman. She worked all the time to support herself and her children. Even so, she still did not earn a living wage. Early in my life, I learned the value of food stamps, food boxes, and other times when a little extra help was needed. I appreciate Social Safety Net programs and remember the feeling of gratitude. I was especially grateful when a single food stamp dollar could buy a box of chocolate doughnuts. That was the best treat in the world! To this day, if I eat a chocolate doughnut, I think of that time in our lives.

My mom was proud when all her children received a high school diploma. Graduating was the bar to meet because she had to drop school at the 9th-grade level to help take care of her brothers and sisters. Years later, she was awarded an honorary high school diploma from a school also named in her honor, Linda Abril Educational Academy (LAEA), after serving 24 years as a school board member in the Phoenix Union High School District (PUHSD). Like the school mascot, the Phoenix, my mother rises from the ashes to a new life.

Despite the many life challenges, she went on to achieve great things. Hers is a story of survival, resilience, and determination. We saw sadness and depression, but whether she meant to or not, we understood these other characteristics and would lean hard on them ourselves. This beautiful, kind woman, who is my mother, did the best she could with her life and with us. When I was 32 years old, she wrote in a letter to me dated 10-28-97: "...just hang in there and take care of you and Vanessa & Tory and try to take one day at a time... I only survived by doing just as I'm telling you now. Don't forget, we all love you and miss you."

DUNG BAG

My mom was physically gone when I was in the third grade, and the memories of feeling abandoned stuck with me. Seeing her in a hospital, being temporarily rehomed, and other emotional ups and downs made it into my Dung Bag (DB). They would resurface in 1992 when I became a mom for the first time. I did not understand depression or know why it could last so long. It was never explained or talked about, so I was left with only confusion and fear that something like that could strike me as well. Given the risk factors, there is such a thing as general depression (Boyles, 2005). This fear increased when I became a single mother with a single income, heartbreaks, and challenges. I thought if I was ever going to break down, please let it not hit me until my girls were beyond third grade. As if that was a measure of success. And yet, when my girls were 16, 14, and seven, the sadness happened to me.

Sibling Rivalry

"Sibling rivalry is particularly intense when children are very close in age and of the same gender..." (Wikipedia, 2021).

SIBLINGS

*T*HREE GIRLS IN THREE YEARS. Then six years later, a baby boy. *My mom could have given us away, but she didn't!* My two older sisters are Joanne and Gigi. I am the baby girl and will forever be known as their little sister. At 325 days apart, Gigi and I are Irish twins. We were asked many times, "Are you twins?" For forty days we are the same age. Joanne is two and one-half years older than me. *They'll always be older than me.* The odds of a beautiful sisterhood were not in our favor.

Our little brother, Roman, is the common ground that brings us together in challenging times. He is the real baby of the family in more than one way. He was born with the congenital disease Down Syndrome ("Downs"), and has developed autistic tendencies throughout his life. Downs is a condition in which a person has an extra chromosome, chromosome 21—also known as trisomy. "This extra copy changes how the baby's body and brain develop, which can cause both mental and physical challenges for the baby." (What is Down Syndrome?, 2021). The "BroMan," as I call him, would never go through the normal developmental growth process. He is now 50 and requires supervision and prompting most of the time. He is the kindest human being I know.

THE ELDEST

Joanne is the older sister. I can't remember a time under my mom's roof when we genuinely got along. It was challenging to look up to her with any admiration. An exception to that is her incredible artistic talents. She has painted a few murals in the Phoenix area, including one at 7th Avenue and Roosevelt, on the Roosevelt side of *El Norteño Restaurant*, titled *"Dios Bendiga Este Negocio"* – God Bless This Business (Wikimedia Commons, 2021). I could never understand why she seemed so angry and aggressive towards us. Throwing a vase at my hip causing a permanent scar is not a nice thing to do. As I said, I never understood her.

As teens, it was not uncommon to be involved in fights and arguments when we were together. There were nights when I awoke from deep sleep to hear shouts and bangs coming from the short hallway in our small John F. Long-built house. *What is going on!* There goes a pan flying across the kitchen to the front door—more holes in the walls.

I would get in between Joanne and my mom or Gigi. I should have worn a Foot Locker shirt as a pajama to be pre-pared to referee the next fight. "Stop it!" I would say as I came out of the bedroom. I recall when I pinned her down in a wrestling hold and demanded that she say she was sorry. I didn't want to punch her or hurt her; I just wanted her to be sorry for fighting with my mom or Gigi. She consented, then I released her. *I didn't see the pair of scissors in her hand until she walked away.* She would have her revenge the following day when I curled my hair before school. Joanne sweeps in with both arms above my head, punches me on the lip, and walks away. My hair was styled, but my lip was on the puffy side. This incident negatively affected my performance at a volleyball game that afternoon. My coach was understanding and said my mom called her to tell her what had happened that morning. I looked up to Coach Mass and always appreciated compassion, minus the embarrassment.

I have no idea what the reasons for the arguments were. Gigi and I would take on the role of mediator and defender, usually between Joanne and my mom. They seemed to happen mostly at night. A significant one occurred during the day while my mom was at work. Again, I had no idea what caused the quarrel, just that it didn't end well for her. I stood about six feet from her staring as she sat on a tan-colored recliner in our living room and cried uncontrollably. Her tearful and snot-dripping face was thumping up and down onto the pillow on her lap. *Why isn't she wiping her face?* It wasn't a physical confrontation; it was an emotional twisting point—for her. *Did I break her? Why did they take her away?* Joanne was admitted to the hospital. This scene is the visual that made it into my DB.

We visited her in a place called the Arizona State Hospital, which provides "quality, compassion, and excellence in the provision of psychiatric care," according to their website (azdhs.gov). They didn't have a website in the early 80s. *It's cold in here, and nobody is smiling.* My mom was quiet and very sad, so was my sister. Compared to my mom's recurring episodes of sadness, Joanne would seem to go in and out of anger. Both would take their paths to wellness and display a resilient and survival mode side to them over the years. *I am glad there was nothing wrong with me.*

FAMILY COUNSELING

Post-hospitalization, there was an attempt to learn how to cope with all the discord at home. It would involve our immediate family. We didn't talk about it much at home, but we had an appointment to meet with a counselor at a local youth center. Metro Youth Center, now replaced with a Circle K convenience store, was a house turned into a youth activity center and conveniently located next to our high school, Trevor G. Browne. It was a cool place to be after school. Students could get help with homework, play games, participate in community activities or hang out. It welcomed students from different ethnic and economic backgrounds and was a social melting pot for youth. *Should I ever win the lottery, I would love to contribute to building a youth center near my kids' high school in Metropolis, Illinois, and give it the same name.*

There were also rooms for individual and family counseling at the center. After going through a difficult episode with my sister Joanne, we were scheduled to meet as a family in one of those rooms. We were there, the counselor was there, but Joanne was not. *She didn't care.* We waited. There she is!

Peering from outside the window and laughing. The counselor said in a hushed tone, "Just ignore her."

Joanne would finish high school at an alternative school setting, the Bostrom Alternative Center in the PUHSD. The Bostrom still helps students complete their high school education (Bostrom Alternative Center, n.d.). After that, she moved out of the house. When she returned a short time later, she wasn't alone. Her son was the cutest baby boy.

Over the next thirty-some years, we have remained distant. When conflict and chaos arise, I remember what that counselor said years ago: ignore her. It is easily done these days with a "block" feature on our mobile devices. I would have embraced a functional relationship with her, but there is uncertainty not knowing which Joanne I'll get, the "What in the hell are you talking about" Joanne, or the one who has her moments of insight and kindness. I feel cheated of a relationship with the latter version. I am left to wonder 'what happened to her?'

THE MIDDLE SISTER

Gigi has always been by my side. She was the one who quietly pulled me from the apartment where Frank lay passed out. Gigi is a protector. She is the reason, and to some extent, Joanne is too, that I don't remember some of the shitty things they carry in their DB. We got along well if I did what she told me to do. Not so much when I didn't. We wouldn't escape the teasing and bickering with siblings, but I don't recall ever having to square up with her. She was a mother figure, and I was the lazy little sister. *You're not my mom; you can't tell me what to do!* Constant commands to help clean the house, be home at a decent hour, and warnings for me to stay out of trouble. Our theme song is "My Life" by Billy Joel. *Go ahead with your own life, leave me alone!*

Her protective nature over me started at a young age. Mother Gigi tells me when she ran alongside my mom, who held me in her arms, rushing from our apartments in the Duppa Villa Housing Project to the nearby St. Luke's Hospital. It was another asthma attack I had. Her worrying nature grew as the years went by, while mine leaned more towards ambivalence. When she was 16 and pregnant, I did not take that so well. I felt scared and mad at the same time. *She's going to leave me.* I knew this was a big deal because two of my uncles came over, picked up my mom and sister, and went to her boyfriend's house to talk with his parents. When they returned, plans for a wedding began. It was all about my sister, and I didn't want any part of that.

The wedding was held at my aunt's house, where we temporarily lived when I was in the third grade. I broke down and asked my sister to forgive me for my terrible attitude towards her. My niece was born in December of 1981, and my nephew followed in May of 1983, making me forever known as Tia Sabrina. Gigi would finish her senior year in a program for teen moms located on the campus of Maryvale High School.

Gigi and I talk about our past and are amazed that we survived. She has her perspective of our lives growing up, the main view of constantly feeling like she had to protect me from what was happening in our home.

Many years later, I would fly from Illinois to Arizona to surprise her for her 30th birthday! That's right; I wouldn't miss an opportunity to tease her for being the first one to turn thirty. Now that we are both on the other side of 55, we are grateful to celebrate each other whether we are together or not.

LITTLE BROTHER

My brother was there for all the dysfunction that rippled through our home environment, seemingly unaffected. He is the silent observer of all that craziness. If he could talk, his story would be a bestseller. Admittedly, I envy his ability to start each day without the weight of the past. Deep down, I also feel cheated of the brother-sister relationships that I often hear about from others. Our relationship is slightly different. I am now his caregiver, and he is my grounding force. Downs has served as a protective factor, shielding him from the traumas surrounding him growing up.

There are exceptions. The phone rang in the early morning hours on April 12, 1993. My firstborn and I were living with my mom at the time. I answered the phone to a distressed voice, "Linda?" "It's Linda's daughter, hold on, and I'll go get her." I woke my mom up to tell her Josie, Frank's first wife, was on the phone. My mom's reaction was quick and was of shock. It was terrible news. Roman's dad was in an accident while driving to his home in Payson, Arizona. This incident was the exception to my brother's emotional connection to a traumatic event. Seeing him hug and pat the closed casket draped with the American flag is forever in my memories.

My poor brother. In the years following, when he thinks of his dad, he points his finger up towards the heavens and says, "Day (for dad), in heaven." This had to be heartbreaking for him and my mom, who I imagine carried the weight of the loss for them both.

Roman loved his visits with his dad. They included eating two eggs, sausage, toast, hash browns, and reading a book or magazine. When those visits stopped, Roman fell into his manner of depression. By then, I had moved back to Georgia, so I didn't see this for myself. Following Frank's death, my mom said a lawyer wanted to interview Roman regarding the death benefits he may receive. She tried to tell the lawyer that Roman would not understand him, but he insisted on speaking to Roman one-on-one. Mom was on standby and could hear Roman repeat, "Day, in heaven," pointing upward with his pointer finger. Bless his heart (the lawyer).

DUNG BAG

Our home environment and the conditions growing up were not ideal. Many risk factors were at play, and they followed us beyond childhood. My sibling relationships varied from sucky to motherly to intellectually disconnected. Bless my mom for doing her best to take care of us while keeping her head above water. I wish I could have been given more knowledge, emotion, and hugs. The lack of these things had me searching to fill the void in all the wrong places and situations. She was a very busy single mom working to keep a roof over our heads and the lights on. The abnormal autopilot was on.

I Don't Like Pills

Mental illness and low self-esteem are listed as major risk factors of teen suicide by the American Association of Suicidology (AAS), (Tracy, 2015).

ATHLETICS

I NEVER SHIED AWAY FROM TRYING OUT FOR A SPORTS TEAM. I even ran for student council vice president in junior high school and won. It was a tie, so I had to share the position with another student, a welcome turn of events. Despite the dysfunction at home, athletics became my escape. I played volleyball, softball, and basketball throughout high school and was a member of the track and field team and varsity cheerleading squad my junior year. Gymnastics was offered as an elective at our high school. I took this class all four years. I dreamed of being in the Olympics. I loved gymnastics, and I had the best teacher, Coach Zamboni. He told me that the machine used to sweep the ice rinks was called a Zamboni. Besides this and so many gymnastics skills, I learned an important life lesson that would become a mantra that I would use and pass on to my children when they faced adversity and challenges.

I spent as much time as I could in the gym. I tried and tried to stick a back Arabian following a round-off back handspring and kept landing on my bottom instead of my feet. It was disorienting and challenging, and I told the coach so. I'll never forget what he said: "It's only hard because you don't know how to do it yet." It's only hard because you don't know how. I've never forgotten that lesson. Over the years, when I don't know how to do something, I think of what he said.

TUMBLING

How is it then that I lost my footing in life? My self-esteem and self-worth took a tumble during my sophomore year in high school. I honestly did not want to do life anymore and was tired of trying to figure things out. *No one would notice I am gone.* I couldn't shake the inner loneliness and feeling of being lost; it became overwhelming. Joanne was gone, Gigi was busy with her husband, my mom was with her boyfriend.

My sister and her husband were out one evening and wouldn't be home until later. I must have been home alone and feeling alone. I called my best friend to talk, but neither of us knew what to do to help the feelings disappear at our age. *Was it the sadness?*

POPPING, ONE-TWO-THREE

I started popping pills. *Maybe these would take away the sadness.* I thought it was the only way to remove my emotional pain; that's all I wanted. I didn't want to feel the weight of whatever it was that I could not understand. If I took many pills, I could go to sleep and never wake up. Although, the only tablets I had available to me were Theo-Dur, a medication to treat my asthma. I took one pill. No problem. Then, I took two more, then three more, and so on. The problem with taking these pills is that they would increase my heart rate to a dangerously fast one. Ironically, I did not think about my heart, only my emotions of loneliness. *Why couldn't I go to sleep?*

When Gigi and her husband returned home, she immediately knew something was wrong with me. She went into mom mode. *She was angry too.* What did you do? What did you take? How many did you take? She seemed mad and concerned at the same time. There were more questions than answers. I believe my sister called our mom and the paramedics. The paramedics arrived, our neighbors came over, my mom showed up, and our small living room was suddenly full of people. Hours before, it was occupied by only me and my loneliness.

People were staring at me, talking at me. *What are they saying?* I don't remember what was said exactly. It wasn't until my neighbor, Sandy, whose children I babysat, convinced me to go to the hospital. I needed to be monitored and receive an IV or something. That was my first experience in an ambulance.

During my short stay, I made a call to a guy, Art, whom I had been talking to on a friendly basis. We didn't talk long. After sharing where I was and why he became short and ended the telephone call. That was it. I couldn't understand why he responded that way. I did not know how to process this except to determine that guys don't care about me. One guy's response was the equivalent of "all" guys. I don't know what I expected. *Maybe I just needed someone to talk to.*

Suicide prevention lines were not available in the eighties. If they were, I wonder if I would have used it. A Wikipedia search indicates that the National Suicide Prevention Lifeline was founded in December 2004 by the Substance Abuse and Mental Health Services Administration (Wikipedia, National Suicide Prevention Lifeline, 2021), 1-800-273-8255 (TALK).

I did have a somewhat funny experience on my next ambulance ride. Not surprisingly, my first job was at a behavioral health agency. It was the umbrella agency to many other entities that provided alcohol, drug, and mental health services. One of the agencies had an ambulance service that responded to overdoses. I volunteered for a ride-along. I didn't know one could overdose on Aspirin? Yeah, it can be a medical emergency. *I still don't like pills.* While on a call, I was asked to get something from the ambulance, and I did not know what or where it was. I brought back an IV bag; it was not what they asked for. *I was so embarrassed.* I learned to say "clear right" in traffic, but clearly, I was wrong in this instance. It was also a good thing it did not interfere with their emergency response. We did a bit of training after that call.

DUNG BAG

I failed. And ever since, despite the many challenges that followed, I am so grateful for this one. It feels like a permanent scar that you don't want to talk about. I thought I wouldn't have to feel anything anymore if I took enough pills. I was willing to accept death. There was no thought about how it would affect my mom, family, friends, or even my coach. Think of all the things I have done, the places I have gone, and my girls. I would not have my children or grandchildren. I still do not like taking pills, and I did not go into the medical field.

Runaway

Before the National Sexual Assault Hotline (1-800-656-HOPE and online.rainn.org) was created in 1994, there was no central place where survivors could get help.

AS BOYFRIENDS GO

J HAD THE BODY AND LOOKS OF SOMEONE OLDER THAN 16. I was fit and firm. I think it had to be the boobs. *Why were older men attracted to me?* With only one boyfriend in high school that lasted only three months, I didn't have much experience. I "talked" to a couple of other guys in high school, but none were public affairs news. Steve broke up with me because I wanted to hang out with another guy who was in town for the weekend. Lance was a football jock who had moved away to another city his senior year. *He wanted to see me!* I told my boyfriend I wanted to see him because we were friends, and he said no. If I did, we would break up.

It was during basketball season, and I was a cheerleader. I snuck out after the game and went with my friend. When he dropped me off at my house, my boyfriend was there waiting. I was so busted. Our boyfriend-girlfriend relationship ended, virginity-intact. I would remain friends with the football jock for many years following, but only on an every-now-and-then, let's-catch-up basis. We lost track of one another about ten years ago.

WEEKENDS

My mom was dating a guy named Craig at the time. Who is this guy? Her male friend lived in an apartment complex with a pool with a volleyball net. Cool! My brother and I went with mom sometimes to hang out and swim. After a couple of weekends playing water volleyball, I became familiar with some guys who lived there. One of them was cute and flirty. I was good at the game and enjoyed the attention. Most weekends, my brother and I would be sent back home, and I would babysit my little brother.

DISCIPLINE

My mom was not a spanker, not because we didn't deserve it. We would get on my mom's last nerve. Maybe she was too worn out at the end of each workday to give two cents. She was in her room a lot, resting. There were times we had to sit through her lectures. Rarely would she lose her temper and scream, but she would never curse. She would only say mother-pucker!

There were exceptions, though, when she had had enough. My sister, Gigi, and I were bickering with each other. I'm sure it was my fault. Suddenly, we run around the kitchen table, trying to get away from our mom. She had an orange Hot Wheels car track in her hand and was yelling and chasing us. I found an opening, ran straight for the bathroom, and locked the door. Neither of them was happy about that. Just outside the door, my sister was pleading with me to open it. I negotiated a 'no spanking' should I open that door. You can guess how that played out.

A SLAP IN THE FACE

My mom was preparing for a solo trip to her boyfriend's house for the weekend. She wanted me to stay home with Roman again. It was just me, mom, and little brother left at home by this time. I had plans, and I did not want to babysit. Didn't she understand? I believed my plans were more important than hers. My smart mouth was activated, and we each began to state our cases, to which my mother had the last word and added a slap to my face. Where did that come from? She never hit us. It was an open-handed slap you see in a dramatic movie scene.

TAKING FLIGHT

For a moment, I stood there frozen and silent. My mom went back to her bedroom to finish packing. I'm outta here. I eyed the front door and saw an escape route. Wearing shorts, a t-shirt, and dollar flip-flops on my feet, I ran out of the house, down the street to the main road, and vanished. I was not going back home, but I did not have a plan.

THUMBS UP

I hitchhiked, as when you stand at the roadside and stick your thumb out to solicit a free ride. What the heck was I doing? A car stopped, and I hopped in with a stranger, a man stranger. Please don't be a killer or pervert. He was kind enough to drive nine miles to my "friend's" apartment. When he dropped me off, he advised me to be careful whom I get rides with. He was a nice guy, but others may not be so trustworthy.

The apartment was easy to find. My "friend" had given me the apartment number during poolside conversations. I was in flight mode, so I didn't think it wise to knock on the front door. Instead, I hopped over the back patio wall and knocked on their sliding glass door. *It felt wrong.* He and his roommate were home, and they let me in. I told my story, the one I had made up, and said I needed a place to crash for a few days. They didn't seem to notice any red flags.

KOS

The cute and flirty one at the pool was called Kos. It was a nickname derived from his last name, Koslowski. That evening we went out to a bar to meet some of his friends. *I'm underage.* The drinking age in Arizona at the time was 19. I was 16. I switched out of my flip-flops into a pair of his closed tennis shoes and wore one of his flannel shirts and hat. *Was I being disguised?* With no purse or identification, Kos vouched for me. We had a couple of drinks and danced before returning to his apartment. I didn't crash on the couch; I ended up in his bedroom.

I've been kissed before, even made out with a boy, but no one was allowed a home run until the night I ran away from home. I should never have run away. He didn't ask if I was a virgin, and I didn't offer a news flash. I only said two words:

be careful. I meant, be careful with me and don't get me pregnant. *We didn't even talk about protection.*

He was surprised the next day when I told him it was my first time. I showed him the evidence. I've heard of cherry popping before but didn't know what that meant. This 23-year-old, man-sized former college baseball player who was over six-feet tall was my first. I was a petite, 16-year, 11-month, and three-days-old runaway. I was also enamored and grateful for a place to stay. He was a man, and that was the night I became a woman-girl. It was like being on alert the whole time; not enjoyable.

HIDING OUT

I hid in their apartment for the next two, three weeks, being careful not to be seen. After a day or two, I took a transit bus back home to pick up some clothes when I knew my mom would be at work. I ran into my neighbor, and he offered me a ride back to my hideout. He gave me some money and assured me he would not tell my mom. That was sure nice of him. I assured him that I would return home in time for a babysitting job for him and his wife. I had committed to them to babysit their kids for a week while his wife traveled to Canada to meet her dad for the first time.

BOREDOM

Oh, Sabrina, Sabrina, Sabrina. What will you do with idle time on your hands? Watch television, smoke cigarettes, and sit back and chill. Don't. Don't do it. Do not go outside and wander around. I just wanted to go to the exercise room at the apartments. I could be invisible; I mean, no one has found me yet. While exercising, a gentleman walked in and said he worked there. He wanted to know if I was a guest and, if so, in what apartment number. Why didn't I lie to protect my cover? It was a freezing moment, and I couldn't think on my feet, so I told him.

The next day there was a knock on the front door. I looked through the peephole and saw my mom and her boyfriend. With resignation, I opened the door and let them in. *I'm totally busted.* They talked, and I listened. Of course, they said they were worried about me and followed with the fact that Kos could be in much trouble because of my age. I told them nothing had happened, that I slept on the couch. *I lied to protect them.* They were kind enough to let me crash at their place, no questions asked. *Maybe they should have asked more questions.*

I was ready to go home, at least looking forward to my week-long babysitting job next door.

DUNG BAG

I didn't know that I would run straight into an adult situation when I ran that day. *I didn't think.* It came at the cost of my virginity. I blamed myself for getting in that situation in the first place. *Why didn't my neighbor tell my mom?* The act of sex did not have any special meaning except that it was my first time. It wasn't love; it wasn't forced, although I felt I had no choice. *I didn't know how to say no.* I didn't know what I was doing, but he did. He was 23, a college graduate, and employed at a bank. I was 16, going on 25, struggling to finish high school. Statutory rape (Wikipedia, Statutory Rape, 2021) made its way into my DB.

Neighborly

Grooming is the process by which an offender draws a victim into a sexual relationship and maintains that relationship in secrecy. The shrouding of the relationship is an essential feature of grooming. (Welner, 2010).

THE COUPLE NEXT DOOR

S'ANDY AND DALE WERE A YOUNG NEWLYWED COUPLE when they had moved into the house next door. Their home was larger and more spacious than ours. *I wish we had a bigger house.* They soon would welcome a baby girl and then a baby boy. Sandy was a lively person and was kind to me. I became a regular babysitter for them. It was great to earn extra money to buy things we otherwise could not afford. I saved up enough money from babysitting to purchase my puffer coat. *I really wanted that coat.* The ones that had removable sleeves and turned into a vest. Very cool!

GROOMING

I became close to the family next door. It was usual to hang out with them even when they did not need me for babysitting. *It was peaceful there.* Sandy taught me how to tuck bed sheets properly, would feed me complete meals, and tried to teach me how to sing. *I can't sing.* The singing didn't work out. I also cut Dale's hair for extra cash. My haircutting skills were not excellent, but he never complained.

One night, after I did my babysitting duties, and as I was leaving, they offered to smoke a joint with me. *How did they know?* A few nights earlier, they may have heard me and my friends passing a joint to each other and laughing in the backyard. So that made it okay, right? Why didn't they *tell my mom?*

I made the cheerleading squad in high school and needed a skirt sewn together. Sandy offered to sew it for me. I thought that was the coolest thing ever and was grateful. *They're such a cool couple.* I enjoyed my mini-runaway trips to the neighbors. Once, Sandy did her best to teach me how to drive a stick shift in her light blue Volkswagen Beetle car. She also gave me advice when I was upset about my sister's teen pregnancy. It seemed like an ideal situation to have a neighbor couple as friends and mentors to help get me through my teen years.

One summer, I went with them to Mexico for a vacation. It would be a babysitting vacation for me, and we would all benefit. Sandy took me shopping for a new bathing suit and said Dale gave her the money to pay for it. *It was a bikini bathing suit.* That was so nice of him. I enjoyed the beach getaway. We all had a great time.

Sandy was not just my neighbor; she was my friend, and I looked up to her. As a housewife, she was full of energy and was helpful with many things my mother did not have the time or energy to do. I liked that about her, but it is not a fair comparison to my mom. Sandy was married and had a husband to support her. *I wish my mom was around more and wasn't so tired.*

SHAME ON HIM

Sandy's sister came to town to attend a wedding. That night, I was babysitting when I heard voices outside. A little concerned, I peeked out the front window to see what was going on. It was Dale and his sister-in-law making out on the front porch. He was cheating on his wife with his wife's sister! *Why are they doing that?* When they came inside the house, they acted as nothing had happened. I never said anything, especially not to Sandy.

SHAME ON ME

After my runaway adventure, I returned to babysit for Sandy and Dale for a week. After all, I made a commitment to them. Sandy had planned a trip to Canada to meet her birth father for the first time. Dale would be home, but he needed help with the kids while at work. They thought it was good for me to stay the night because Dale left so early for work in the morning. It would be more convenient, and I could sleep on the couch. *I didn't mind.*

On the first night, I awoke when I felt someone touching my body. It was Dale kneeling next to me. *What the...* He told me that he was disappointed that he wasn't my "first" and waited a long time to be with me. *Did I disappoint him?* Lightening thoughts streaked through my head from what his hands were doing. *I can't leave; the kids are sleeping. What's happening.* He picked me up, carried me to his bedroom, and was confident we wouldn't get caught because he had a vasectomy. *Did that make it okay?* What about Sandy? He wouldn't tell if I didn't speak.

It was a long week playing house with Dale. When Sandy returned home, I was happy to get back home to my mom. I didn't tell her what had happened. *What if Sandy finds out?* It would not be the last time Dale and I were together. After several months, Sandy became suspicious that something was going on between us. She talked to my mom about it. My mom spoke to me about it. *If I denied it, would that make the reality of what had happened to go away?* No, Mom, we're just friends. He was there to listen to me when I had some problems.

IN PURSUIT

I should have known it was wrong. Dale would pursue me throughout my senior year of high school. I was 17 by then, and he was 24, and he gave male attention to this woman-girl. It was not the kind of attention a married man should give to his babysitter.

He took me to odd places for the specific purpose of having sex, including a dive motel and out in the middle of a field. By this time, the sex act had become numb and void of emotions. I remember the shock of pornography showing on the motel room television. *Is this normal?* It seemed adventurous at the time but, in retrospect, was very demeaning.

Dale even showed up at my high school. *Why is he here?* I was hanging out with a friend at some tables in the quad when we both heard someone shouting my name from the direction of the parking lot. "Sabrina!" I turned around to see Dale walking toward me. Dan asked, "who is that?" I said, "nobody, but I gotta go!" I gathered my stuff, turned, and headed towards Dale to stop him from coming any further. I did not want anyone to know who he was and why he was there for me.

DUNG BAG

The encounters with Dale were not many, but they should never have taken place. *I still feel so guilty.* He should have known better not to engage with a vulnerable, underage family friend and babysitter. I lost my friendship with Sandy, and she and Dale divorced. *Why didn't I stop him the first time?* Sandy and the kids kept the house and continued to live next door to my mom for several years; until they finally moved.

Two weeks after graduating high school, I moved out of my mom's house. *I had to get away.* Conflicting emotions would surface each time I would return home to visit my mom. That house was still next door, and it reminded me that something meaningful twisted into something sick and wrong. It wasn't love; it wasn't forced; although I knew it wasn't right, I felt trapped. If I had told Sandy, it would cause her so much pain. *Or maybe she wouldn't believe me.* This whole experience became a significant DB dump.

PERSONAL REDEMPTION

About seven-eight years later, I saw him at a concert. *Is that Dale?* I worked at the venue and had just clocked out. He was in the audience. Dale wanted to call me, so I gave him my phone number. *Why did I give him my number?* Over the next couple of days, I had a chance to think. The awful memories came flooding back, and so did the disturbing emotions; it made me sick to think about what we had done together and what it had done to his family. Now, with the knowledge of a 24-year-old woman-girl, I understood more that the sexual encounters we had were inappropriate. It was wrong and harmful to me, Sandy, and his children.

I received his call at work. *I bet he wants to get together.* He wanted to get together. I was prepared. There is a saying, "when you know better, you do better." This time I chose to do better. I told him that what he had done to me back then was wrong and that I would not meet with him now or ever. *Take that, you man jerk!* This decision was liberating and gave a little closure to that chapter of my life. *I still carry the guilt.* I have never seen or spoken to him again.

Birth Certificate Guy

In 1965, 24 percent of black infants and 3.1 percent of white infants were born to single mothers. By 1990 the rates had risen to 64 percent for black infants, 18 percent for whites. Every year about one million more children are born into fatherless families. (An analysis of out-of-wedlock births in the United States, 1996).

FATHER FIGURE

MY MOM WAS MARRIED TO MY LITTLE BROTHER'S DAD for a short while. *Did they have a wedding?* We lived as a family for a short time. As a family, we camped in the mountains and swam at the Phoenix Air National Guard, or PANG club, as I remember it. For a short while. My sisters have a better recollection of our time together with Frank. *Except for that one afternoon.*

My sisters and I had a different dad who never lived with us or visited us. *Did he not love us?* We knew of him by way of a back alley to his work, presumably, so my mom could collect money from him. George wore a cowboy hat and boots and was a dark-skinned Mexican American Indian round-bellied man. *He looked like a fierce Indian chief.* So, we knew what he looked like, but we didn't know his character.

My mom seldom dated, and none stuck around long enough to be of any significance. There was Frank T. who would come around throughout the years. *We all liked him.* He is the one who left a positive impression on me. I played volleyball in high school but did not have the money to buy the cool flat-soled volleyball shoes like the other players on the team wore. He was visiting my mom one day when I came home from practice. He must have heard me asking my mom about volleyball shoes. After he left, my mom said he gave her $50 for me to buy those shoes. *I was so excited and grateful for this.* He was a teacher, and that day I was a student on the receiving end of a lesson of kindness.

I recall Roman's dad would pick him up for his bi-weekly visitation. Roman was always so happy to see his dad. *Why didn't our dad come to see my sisters and me?* It was just for the day, but Frank still came to see his son. Frank would continue to see Roman until he died in 1993.

GEORGE, SR.

George had a family before fathering three daughters with my mother. He already had two sons and a daughter with his first wife, Barbara. *Was he still married to her?* I shared a birthday with his other daughter, although she is much older than me. His oldest son was his namesake and was called Junior. David was his second son. They seemed more familiar with their dad than we were with ours.

I knew George worked at a used car lot in the Phoenix downtown area. This job is, perhaps, why he promised us, girls, a car when we turned 16. *That never happened.* Besides being named as the father on my birth certificate, he was the same man who took us to visit our mom in the hospital many years earlier.

MOCKINGBIRD

"...for the second time in my life, I thought of running away..." writes Jean Louise "Scout" Finch in *To Kill a Mockingbird*. I ran away the first time the summer between my junior and senior years. That same summer, I would run again.

I continued to feel restricted and trapped at home. *The neighbor thing didn't help matters.* This time I ran towards George's car lot on Van Buren Street. I hitchhiked again. *It was safe the first time, and I was on the run again.* After a 12-mile ride with a man-stranger, I showed up at this "dad" of mine's place of employment. I confidently told him, "You are my dad, and you should take care of me now." *Why was I such an unhappy teen?*

UNDERAGE DRINKING

The first thing George does is take me to a bar. *Why are we going to a bar?* I was only 17, and Arizona's drinking age was still 19 (the year I turned 19, the legal drinking age was changed to 21 by the Arizona State Legislature). We sat at the bar, where he ordered alcoholic drinks for both of us. *Did I eat anything before I ran?* Not even an attempt at a Shirley Temple drink for me.

Straight to the point, he asked me if I was a virgin—a strange question to ask your runaway daughter. I told him the truth. It would have been a different answer just a few weeks ago. He then asked me if I liked oral sex. *What the hell is oral sex?* I was new to this sex stuff and didn't know what he was talking about, so I said, "Nah, I don't like that." He seemed to suggest that if done right, I would. "Nah, dad, I'm good." This man was supposed to be my dad; why were we having this conversation.

We had more to drink until I became a bit disoriented. *I think my lips are numb.* I needed some fresh air, so I stepped outside. *I gotta get the heck out of here.* We left the bar, and before we got out of the parking lot, I had to vomit. He slowed the car enough for me to open the door, stick my head out, and throw up whatever I had been drinking. *Why did he let me drink alcohol?* I don't know what I expected him to do with me or that he knew what to do with his teenage daughter showing up at his doorstep. Maybe I could crash on his couch for a bit. Instead, he took me to a hotel room.

THAT HOTEL ROOM

It was still daylight when we arrived at the hotel room, and I needed to lay down. *I'm not feeling so well.* I felt the effects of the alcohol and vomiting but was not passed out. George got on the bed, too. *What!* Then, he began to rub my back. *What the hell is he doing?* I froze. When he unsnapped my bra, I jumped up and out of bed. *WTF!* I moved to the chair and tried to figure out what to do. He was still lying in bed. I asked him if I could have some quarters to make a call to my girlfriend. I went for a walk and found a payphone. It was the same friend I called when I was feeling hopeless. *Thank good-*

ness she answered the phone. We talked a little, and again, we both did not know what to do in this situation. *Should I tell her what happened?* I don't believe I told her what happened until many years later.

When I returned to the hotel room, I asked George if I could use his car to see my friend. He said no, and then got out of bed and left for the night. *Thank goodness he didn't stay.* I was relieved to see him go. I stayed the rest of the night by myself.

HALF BROTHERS

George returned to the hotel room the next day. *Is he going to send me home?* He was taking me to stay with Barbara, his first wife and the mother of his first set of kids. Barbara stayed home, and her two sons lived there too; they were around 19 and 24. I saw them come and go all day and night. *I didn't have a life.* All the bedrooms were occupied, leaving me to camp out on the couch. George quickly abdicated parental responsibility to his former wife and then left me inserted into this new family of unfamiliarity. At least I wasn't at home, right.

BIG SURF

David, the younger of the brothers, had company one afternoon. We were both sitting in the living room making small talk. I knew there was something familiar about his friend but couldn't immediately pinpoint what it was. It took us a minute before we realized that we had met before. He was the guy who had buried his feet in the sand next to mine as we flirted with each other when a high school girlfriend and I were at Big Surf. He didn't know I was his best friend's little sister; I didn't know that either. He asked me not to say anything to David. So, I didn't.

A few nights later, the Big Surf guy secretly invited me to his house around the block within walking distance. *Okay, I'm bored, so I'll go.* Mr. Merriam and Mr. Webster would define this encounter as a quickie. *Why did I let him have sex with me?* It wasn't love, it wasn't forced, although this time, I had an idea that was a possibility. *Is that all men want, sex?* It was another sexual encounter that left me void of emotion and stunned by the short-lived attraction and attention. I don't know why I thought it was a good idea. He asked me not to say anything to David. So, I didn't.

THE HEARSE

I walked around the neighborhood when I was not on the couch watching television. One afternoon I picked up a job application at Wendy's and was told I needed to get a food handler's card. *How do I do that?* I walked a lot. While walking on a hot summer day, I caught a man's attention in a white tow truck. He asked me if I wanted to go with him on a job to pick up a broken-down vehicle. It supposedly wasn't far and wouldn't take long. What else did I have to do? So, I hopped in.

We traveled from the east side of town to the west side past my mom's house on I-10 in the direction of California. *Where is he taking me?* We didn't cross the state line, but to me, it was far. He turned off the freeway onto a dirt road. I thought, okay, I am going to die in the desert. I took a deep breath of relief when we approached a broken-down vehicle at last.

Before leaving the middle-of-nowhere, desert scene, he paused. *Oh my, this is where I die.* He started to touch my hair and caress my upper body. He wanted me to do the same to him but on his lower body. *I don't want to have sex.* I told him I did not want to have sex. I am most grateful that he complied with my request. He then made me feel him, or rather, his member. He pulled my head down and forced my face and mouth down on him. *This was gross.* That's what oral sex is. I was right, I do not like it.

We made it back to the interstate and headed back to the city. On the way, the tow truck got a flat tire. We pulled over safely, and he determined that the tow truck was undrivable. So, we stuck our thumbs out for a free ride. *Why did I hop in his truck?* It was almost sunset, so we were grateful when a car finally stopped and offered us a ride, even if it was a hearse, a loaded hearse. An older gentleman drove it. The tow guy sat in the back with the deceased, and I sat in the passenger's seat. The hearse guy dropped me off a couple of blocks from Barbara's house, and I walked from there. When I returned from being gone all day, no one seemed to miss me or even asked where I had been.

GEORGE, JR.

The namesake. George, Jr. was born in 1957, so he was eight years older than me, his little half-blood sister—I was born in 1965. It was 1982. Junior was big and taller than me, and he was friendly, though not too talkative.

After a night of drinking, he came home and woke me up from my sleep on the couch. He said he wanted to watch television and told me I could sleep on his bed in his room. He said, take my bed, and I'll sleep out here on the couch. I got up from the sofa, went to his room, and fell back to sleep.

I woke up later when I felt a body crawling into the bed, pulling the blankets off me. *What's happening?* It was Junior. I felt the weight of his body only for a moment as I wriggled out of his bed. I made it back to the couch and tried to stay alert for the rest of the night. It wasn't love, and it was plotted and planned by a drunk half-blood brother. The next day, he told me he was sorry and only did that because he was drunk. *Right.* I was on high alert for the remainder of my stay.

DUNG BAG

If a father could entertain the idea of having sex, any kind of sex, with his daughter, then I don't need one. I was certainly better off not having him take care of me the first 17 years of my life. This experience makes me grateful for my mother regardless of how unhappy I felt.

I am disgusted and haunted by what he attempted. And to top off the family affair, his son inherited his sick sexual madness. These two men caused one of the most long-lasting post-traumatic effects in my life. I am glad I knew enough that family members should not be doing that kind of stuff and stopped it and that they did not finish what they started.

I only wish these *Jorge-istic* experiences could have stayed in the DB, but they would creep into and interfere with my future courtships, especially when I found myself in long-term relationships. It would take an enormous amount of work and trust to overcome.

George sent me back home at the end of the summer so I could finish my senior year. *I am glad he did.* He would show up again to attend my high school graduation in 1983. *As if to take credit for the accomplishment.* We went to dinner afterward. It would be several years before I would see him again, not by choice.

He was a patient at a skilled care facility and deteriorating from Lou Gehrig's disease. My mom and sister, Gigi, wanted me to go with them to see him. *Don't they know what a creep he is?* They didn't understand why I didn't want to go see a dying man. *He's your dad!* Neither wanted to believe or hear what had happened when I tried to explain. I succumbed to their request and went with them. There was no love, it was forced, and it was another opportunity for me to practice emotional detachment. *That bastard!* May he rest in peace.

PART II

Woman–Girl

THESE CHAPTERS ARE RECOLLECTIONS of my experience out on my own and through my twenties. They recount specific events that shaped my views of men, marriage, and commitment.

I WAS A FUNCTIONAL, WORKING ADULT. I did not recognize that heavy drinking was a way to hide the pain. Having family, friends, and sometimes strangers watch over me to make sure I made it home safely was a blessing. I said "I do" twice! Once at 19 and then at 26. I became a mother at 27 and 28. My marriage experiences could have been better, but they also could have been worse. I could have been a stronger person, but I could have been weaker.

WHAT MATTERS IS THAT I AM ALIVE AND WELL.

My First "I Do"

People do not get married planning to divorce. Divorce is the result of a lack of preparation for marriage and the failure to learn the skills of working together as teammates in an intimate relationship. —Gary Chapman (GreetingIdeas.com).

MY OWN PLACE

M_Y BEST FRIEND SINCE SEVENTH GRADE AND I MADE_ plans to share an apartment right after graduating from high school. I found a job quickly at Community Behavioral Services, a health agency where my aunt worked. Full-time receptionist, making a whopping five dollars an hour. My skill set: I could type fast, use shorthand to take dictation quickly, and I was a fast learner. I wanted out of my mom's house, her neighborhood, and my memories there. I signed a lease right away and moved into a one-bedroom apartment in June of 1983.

This decision was a selfish move on my part. *Why did I want to be alone?* I left my mom at home with my little brother, and I missed out on an opportunity to live with my best friend. Over the years, I never did end up living with her. We're still best friends and have been for over 40 years. *I don't know what I would do without her.*

LOOK AT ME NOW

I finally had a place of my own where I could rest my head and know that I could sleep in peace. There was no waking to my mom and sister fighting and no grown men crawling into bed unwelcomed. It was easy to explain it if I felt alone because I lived alone. It was my haven.

I worked, played, and cleaned my place. I received two surprise visitors while living in my first apartment. That guy from high school, Lance, whom I snuck off with after the basketball game, sought me out. *He came to see me.* He was too cool for me in high school, and now he is the one seeking me out, but we remained only friends.

Dale also showed up. *What was he doing here?* I was cordial, but I made sure his visit was brief. He got the message that I had moved on.

Lance said he found out where I lived from my mother. I don't know how Dale found me.

The apartment complex had tennis courts, a pool, and a sand volleyball court as features. Many single adults lived there. I would be 17 for another month, and then I would become a full 18-year-old adult woman-girl. I was a regular at the volleyball court and was a skilled player on the sand. There are many sunny days throughout the year for outdoor activity in Phoenix. Overall, I was having fun and living my life my way.

After living there for nearly a year, I caught this guy's eye. We began to flirt with each other during the volleyball games. *He was impressed with my volleyball skills.* I began to look forward to seeing him on the weekends when residents and their guests gathered to swim and play ball.

Steve and I began dating in 1984. He took me to see the movie *Against All Odds*, a title that became a prediction of our future. He was living at home with his mom and dad at the time. We moved into an apartment together and became engaged in just a short time. We set a wedding date for April of 1985. I was 19, and he was 21. *I'm old enough to get married, right?* College was not on my radar. I've lived independently for a year and believed I was ready to move on to the next chapter of life. *I had no idea what steps to take in life.*

I could have picked one of my uncles to walk me down the aisle, but I chose my mother. *She raised me.* We got married in a church, and my Nana's pastor officiated. We made promises to love and cherish each other before family and friends as witnesses and under the eyes of God and his house. *I believed we would be married for life.* The reception was in my mom's backyard. It was one of the few times our yard had green grass and looked landscaped. *We rarely had green grass in our yard.*

My family made tacos, rice, and beans, and his family brought potato salad and coleslaw. We had two beer kegs since we had different tastes: Budweiser and Coors. The mariachis were a must. The use of cocaine throughout the night was not. *Why was this a thing?* Thus we started our marriage.

HIS FAMILY

I was new at commitment. New at cooking and cleaning, and new at long-term healthy sexual relations. *There was drinking involved a lot of the time, that helped.* We were an actual couple. He was from a family of couples. Four of his five siblings were already married; the other was engaged. He was the youngest of six and still lived at home. *I stepped onto the Brady Bunch set.*

His dad, Dr. Jarvis, was a high school science teacher at Maryvale High School. Steve and I went to rival high schools. Juanita, his mom, was a homemaker. Their family aura was unfamiliar; it was calm and opposite of mine. Culturally, our families were different, but Steve and I found shared interests and fell in love anyway. I was entering a picture-perfect nuclear family. *It felt like a shadow of perfection overhead.*

ADVENTUROUS

We worked to support ourselves, paid our bills, and had enough funds to enjoy the extras, like beer, drugs, toys, and pets. We were adventurous. Our honeymoon cruise to Mexico was fun. We had a blast joining the science club on camping trips where we hiked and crawled in caves; we would go on weekend getaways and even made a trip to Disneyland for our second anniversary. We got a three-wheeler for each other for our first anniversary. The same one I broke my collarbone on when Steve reached around and pulled on the brakes, causing a rollover accident on Hutch Mountain near Mormon Lake. *It was his fault!*

We also drank on the weekends, smoked pot, and tested plenty of other illegal recreational drugs: cocaine, mushrooms, and even a "hit" of acid (once, and that was enough). Steve had a close friend, his best man at our wedding, who may have been a dealer of the drugs. *May he rest in peace.* Steve was a functional pothead, never missed work, and was, not surprisingly, a very chill dude.

I didn't smoke much because of my asthma. Eventually, the drinking and other drug use became exhausting for me. It affected my health and caused missed workdays. I was not as chill; I was still missing something, and I couldn't pinpoint what that was.

In Arizona, adult use of recreational marijuana was legalized by voters in November 2020, becoming the 15th state to legalize it. *Party on Steve!*

OUR HOUSE

After apartment living, we rented a house around the corner from my mom. Then we purchased our own home with the help of Steve's older brother, Scott, who was a pothead too and a very chill kind of guy. *Not so perfect family, after all.* It was a lovely house with plenty of space, three bedrooms and *two* bathrooms, and a two-car garage! We even had a dog, a cat, and two birds.

To pay for this house, I worked at a law firm where I learned many new skills: bond financing, legal documentation, jargon, and computer skills. It was a professional atmosphere, where I notarized documents at closings, prepared legal forms and processed billable hours. *Attorneys charge high fees per hour.* It was like getting paid to attend school, on-the-job learning. Steve worked for a printing company and ran a large printing press for a decent salary. His goal was to become a pressman journeyman and make much more money.

DON'T TOUCH ME!

We started to disagree with each other more and more. First, it was little things, then more serious problems. I was tired of weekend drinking and wanted Steve to stop smoking pot daily. *I didn't want to do that anymore.* This new perspective was not well received. One time the arguing turned to an altercation. I probably should have kept my mouth shut.

I heard his footsteps coming back down the hallway and towards the living room, where I sat after our argument. He came after me with his words and hands. *Is he...?* I believe he thought he was going to get the best of me. Up until this moment, I had no reason to think he would ever lay his hands upon me. He grabbed me tightly by the arms and began to swing at me. I caught a few swings on my arms, fell back on the couch, and brought my legs up to defend myself. I countered his screams and shouts with the shouting of my own and the kicking of my legs. Then it stopped and went quiet, except for the heavy breathing that comes following a wrestling match.

MARRIAGE COUNSELING

Before getting married, we attended pre-marital counseling with the pastor. We made an appointment with a catholic social services organization for marital counseling this time. Neither of us had the disposition to forgive our mutual trespasses or the willingness to budge on our ultimatums. *We both had our demands to move forward.* You must want to resolve or compromise on your differences for counseling or mediation to work. *This session was a mediation, not counseling.* Instead, it was, stop smoking pot, or that's it, or go to Wednesday dinners, or that's it. And that was it.

LEARNING CURVE

We wouldn't recover from that single altercation. *I won't let you hit me again.* We both walked away from each other, learning something new. Me: Men are not to be trusted, even those who make life-long promises to love and cherish. Him: Never, ever, lay a hand on your wife again!

Apologies and marriage counseling didn't work, and new wedding rings wouldn't work. A few months prior, we had upgraded our wedding rings. *Material things do not make a marriage work.* Before splitting up, I talked with Steve's parents to see if they could help by talking to him. That didn't work either. I hoped that we could recover from our differences about marriage and our future, but it was not to be. *Thank goodness we didn't have kids.*

My new skills from the law firm came in handy. I swiftly drew up a complete set of divorce papers, divided the property, had them signed and filed. This move saved us both loads of attorney fees. He was a higher-wage earner, so he got to keep the house and dog. I got to fully furnish a one-bedroom apartment and live alone again with my peace.

DUNG BAG

Being married to Steve was not a total loss. I gained a few life lessons, none so heavy as what was already in my DB. I thought being married would give me a shield of safety and protection. I never considered compromises, ultimatums, or anymore unwanted physical contact. However, in the end, there were no hard feelings either. Over the years, when I hear the song by Phil Collins, *Take a Look at Me Now*, I can't help but think of him for a moment. There are no tears left for him; I only nervously laugh when I think about that time.

My Choice

For women who know they're pregnant, about 10 to 15 in 100 pregnancies (10 to 15 percent) end in miscarriage. (Miscarriage, 2017).

POST-DIVORCE LIFE

*J*SETTLED INTO MY NEW PLACE AND BEGAN A NEW LIFE with no husband, no dog, and no idea what direction it would go. I was 22 years old, suddenly back to a single income and a single lifestyle. *Because I've lived such a long life already.* I was restless and needed a plan.

If I had gone to college after high school, I would have finished by now. *Not one teacher talked to me about college, not even my mother.* My mom was proud of us girls for achieving our high school education. But I wanted to continue my post-secondary education after taking two-night classes during my marriage with Steve. Instead, it was working to pay bills. Education was secondary. *Why did I move out of my mom's house?* My salary as a legal secretary allowed me to save up enough money to take three classes and purchase textbooks.

So, I switched jobs to work at night for another law firm in the word processing department and attended college.

COLLEGE GIRL

There was no college dorm room experience for me. I lived on my own and had to manage my work and school schedules. When I studied at the community college, I ran into some folks from my past. Some people from high school, one of Steve's friends (because you don't keep the same friends when you divorce), and I even ran into my older sister, Joanne. She was taking art classes. I asked her how she was able to pay for college, and she told me about these grants that helped her. *I wish I knew about grants.* I didn't know what a grant was.

While walking around campus, I found myself in the gym watching the volleyball team warming up for a game. *I wish I could play.* The scheduled game was forfeited for lack of enough players, so I jumped in to offer my skill set. It was an unofficial game, and I was able to keep up. Even though it didn't count, it was excellent!

THE ARTIST

I made it through one semester and was unable to pay for another. I switched jobs again and began work at another law firm, processing edited documents for lawyers. I was the new girl at work, and I caught the eye of a cute, friendly mailroom guy. It started with bits of flirting and then small conversations. *It always starts with small talk.* He had a great personality and was a very talented artist. We would soon plan the first date but would have to keep it a secret because the work gossip train would take off quickly. *Why am I always a secret?*

Bill was so sweet and fun to be with. I enjoyed his artwork, and he enjoyed being with me. Then I missed a period and began to worry that I was pregnant. That worry was confirmed in a phone call while I was at work. We both were waiting anxiously for the results of the blood test. I picked up the phone and dialed his extension and, with a whispered voice, told him, "It's positive."

DECISIONS, DECISIONS

We met after work to talk about what comes next. Neither of us was in a place financially or emotionally to start a family, but we would be okay with whatever decision was made, including the abortion option. We were both open to that as a possible alternative. But I was raised catholic. *What would my mom think?* When my sister had an unplanned teen pregnancy, abortion was not even on the table.

I lived in a large house with my sister, niece, nephew, and another friend who went to high school with us. I had plenty of counsel. I had known others who chose abortion and fared well. It was their best decision, and I needed to make my best decision now.

My decision: keep the baby and take responsibility. I would not get married, however. Bill would make a great co-parent, and we would be all right for the time being.

VIABILITY

I hadn't even made it to my first doctor's appointment when I started spotting. It was a weekend, so my sister and friends were available to accompany me to the nearby hospital emergency room for a checkup. The lab work determined that the pregnancy was still viable. They told me to make an appointment with my OB/GYN immediately.

The following two weeks were an up-and-down situation. More lab work revealed that I might be losing the baby—*the baby*. I thought of it as a baby because I had accepted that I would welcome him or her into this world. Finally, the human chorionic gonadotropin (hCG) levels decreased to the point that confirmed a miscarriage. My body made a different decision than I had.

The miscarriage required a procedure for dilation and curettage (D&C) at a Maryvale hospital. I did not choose abortion. Miscarriage, or spontaneous abortion, chose me.

SEVERANCE

An appointment for the D&C procedure was set for a Wednesday so that I could have Thursday, Friday, and the weekend to recover. My nurse was Lance's mother, my high school friend whom I've kept an on-again-off-again friendship with. I was a bit nervous and comforted at the same time. Bill came over the evening of the procedure to check on me. He brought flowers and didn't know what else to do or say. He had a kind soul.

I planned to keep the miscarriage a secret. I called in sick for those three days and returned the following Monday. Immediately, they told me to go to HR. Either the secret got out, or it was rather odd timing for the law firm to decide they were letting me go. They gave me my paycheck and three-week severance pay. I went home to rest and to update my resume.

By the third week of no employment, I had secured a job with a national non-profit agency on the east side of town. My new boss, Major Hogan! I would learn new skills in this new job: property, contract, and program business documentation for the second in command of headquarters. I would also volunteer to serve meals on Christmas morning, volunteer at the women's shelter, and learn about being born again.

DUNG BAG

It's hard to say how life would have turned out had my body been able to carry the pregnancy to full term. *Was the baby a boy or a girl?* He or she would be around over 30 years old now. I wonder about this only sometimes. Bill and I went our separate ways after this experience. Later I learned that miscarriage is so common. However, that doesn't make it less of a loss for anyone. It also comes up when filling out past medical history forms for doctor's offices. Four pregnancies, three births.

Date Night

"Tis a lesson you should heed, try, try again.
If at first you don't succeed, try, try, and try
again." —Edward Hickson's *"Moral Song."*

A NEW PLACE

*B*Y 1990 I HAD MOVED INTO MY OWN PLACE AGAIN—a one-bedroom in the same apartment complex where my sister and cousin lived. *I enjoyed living with my sister and her kids.* I was still working at a non-profit agency and taking another night class. The latest course was Accounting since I thought I wanted to be an accountant during that semester.

I worked, went to school, did homework, poolside, played volleyball, lived in my own space, and partied on the weekends. *My method of coping was alcohol.* Life was moving on. I frequented a local bar, Chubbie's, within walking distance from my apartment. Several residents would walk to Chubbie's and safely walk back home after a night of fun and shooting pool, drinking, and throwing darts. It was a cool local social hangout.

THIS GUY

A guy seemed to be there almost every time I was. He had a larger-than-life personality and was very good at darts, being the center of attention, and drinking. He had a bad-ass, tough-guy-from-Chicago attitude. Everyone knew him, and hardly anyone would mess with him. Until he made a derogatory remark to my date one night. He joked about his softball cleats and may have said something about them being faggot shoes. They started to square off when I got in between them to stop the stupid fight. *Not cool, dude!*

A DIFFERENT GUY

I was there another night, waiting on a date to arrive. I sat at Chubbie's alone for a while when that guy from Chicago sat down across from me. At first, it was small talk, and I told him I was waiting for a date. *He sure was bold.* It didn't bother him that I was waiting for someone else. When my date arrived, he went back to playing darts, and I continued the night with my date. We had fun shooting pool.

I forget my date's name, but that Chicago guy's name was Vince, or Vinnie, by all who knew him in Arizona. Vince's small talk leveled up to flirting throughout the night. When I would go up to the bar to get a drink, he would talk to me. He was overly friendly on this occasion, and it was hard not to notice.

It was no surprise that my date left early. I stuck around to talk to Vince a bit more. We closed the bar and went back to his place to talk more. He lived just a few doors down from my sister. She remembers him as being a loud party animal and would get irritated at his late-night parties.

We had both been married and divorced. Vince and his first wife tried to start a family but couldn't. He told me he would not be able to have kids. *I believed him.* I should have known he was full of poop when he went militaristic and said he couldn't say too much about his job. I wasn't on a need-to-know basis, plutonium this and uranium that, and if he told me, he'd have to kill me. All in fun, and we had a good laugh. I was getting tired, so he walked me back to my apartment and left me at my front door without as much as a kiss or handshake. *This guy is a gentleman.* He left me with the impression that underneath that lively persona was a very nice guy.

COURTSHIP

He took me to see the movie *The Godfather* for our first date. I remember this so well because I spilled my large soda on his lap near the movie's beginning. We stayed anyway. I was so sorry, and he was still very cool about it. He worked the night shift as a crew chief on F-16 fighter jets at Luke Air Force base in Arizona. I worked days and would go to a night class once a week. We tried to meet at Chubbie's on the weeknights when he got off work at 11:00 p.m. I met him as much as I could but couldn't stay too long because I had to work early in the morning.

It wasn't long before we were a couple. Everyone at Chubbie's knew I was Vinnie's girlfriend. That made me feel special since he was so well-liked. *Some people didn't like him.* My sister didn't care much for him. Her proximity to Vince's apartment and the loud late-night parties bothered her since she had kids and had to get up early for work. I joined his parties and wasn't spending as much time with my family anymore. However, I did bring him home for Thanksgiving dinner. We went to see his grandma in Tucson for Christmas. *He told me to call him by a different name in front of her.*

I did my best to keep up with him. We hung out, and I adapted to his work schedule. *He didn't adapt to mine.* We never got to the point of moving in with each other, and I was grateful for that. I still needed my own place for rest and quiet.

LOVE TKO

I finished my accounting class at the end of 1990; however, it would not be until 1998 that I returned to post-secondary education. After the holidays, Vince received orders for a one-year tour of duty in South Korea and was to report in March of 1991. He left at the end of January to visit his mom and dad in Illinois before heading overseas. We said goodbye at the Phoenix Sky Harbor International Airport.

VISITING ILLINOIS

Neither of us could leave well enough alone. It wasn't long before Vince called to invite me to visit him at his parent's house in Illinois. *I would love to see him again.* I was more than willing to fly out there to see him one more time. Nashville, Tennessee, was the nearest airport. He and his parents picked me up at the airport, and we drove back to his hometown. His parents were very welcoming and embraced me immediately. *Why are they calling him Phillip?*

We drove through Paducah, Kentucky. Is this it? No. We went through Metropolis, Illinois. Is this it? No. The scenery was beautiful, much different from Arizona's dry brown deserts. There were so many green trees and lots of grass. These views reminded me of when I would go camping in the mountains with Steve. But people lived and worked here. I was amazed. We arrived at his parents' house in the village of Joppa, Illinois, population 492.

Vinny from Chicago was from Chicago as much as he was from Chicago by the way of Joppa. The time lived in each place while divided unequally is not relevant. I always say I am from Arizona, even though I've lived in Illinois for 27 years. So, we are from wherever we say we are from. He had determined his post-high school identity would be as a Chicagoan. Indeed, his mom's family was from Chicago, as was his biological father. The dad he lived with and raised him —the real Vince— was from West Virginia. Everyone who was not from Arizona kept calling my Vince by another name, Phillip.

Vince's mom was also not a doctor, as he told me. She worked at a doctor's office. His dad, whose name he hijacked, worked at a coal terminal. They were a hardworking, fun-loving, loud-voiced family. In stark contrast to mine, their everyday communication with each other was robust. You couldn't tell the difference between dialogue and disagreement, which left me uncomfortable and on guard at times. Perhaps our families' contrast lay in the differences between the Italian and Mexican cultures or the two-parent and single-parent environments.

PHILLIP

Who in the hell is Phillip? They knew him as Phillip, but I knew him as Vince or Vinny from Chicago. In all fairness, Phillip was his name. Charles was his middle name given to him at birth and was his birth dad's name. He had a name change when his stepdad —now dad— adopted him. Phillip sure was proud of his new name, DeMarco! He was also conflicted with the birth name he left behind. But that's his story to tell if only he could. While it was odd to me, it was reasonable that everyone in Illinois kept calling him Phillip. *I still called him Vince, or Vincent, when I was mad.* I called him Vincent a lot.

PEOPLE AND PLACES

I got to meet his extended family and a few friends. They were just as welcoming and happy to see him. His parents took us to the Garden of the Gods in the Shawnee National Forest, and it was amazing. I had been to the Grand Canyon before, but this was a different kind of grand. We ate a steak dinner at the local Elks Lodge that Vince (the dad) was a member of. Of course, Vince and I got out at night to have fun and drinks.

We went to the bar near his home in Joppa on one of those nights. It was called the Knotty Pine. It was a small, dark place, unlike the bar that the birth certificate guy had taken me to years ago. After a couple of shots, we locked down a marriage commitment to each other. It went something like this: "Will You Freakin' Marry Me?" I accepted on the spot. *I didn't need a ring, right.*

Vince would still go on his tour of duty overseas, but I was happy to see him one more time. There was no engagement ring, no photo op, no real marriage plan. *Just wait for me until I get back.* I was on lockdown for a year with a single question asked and a single answer given. I can adapt and overcome.

WHEN THINGS CHANGE

I failed to adapt and overcome. We wrote letters to each other for months, but I became restless. After Vince left, I tried to keep busy. Instead of partying at Chubbie's, I worked there. After four nights, the owner sat me down and suggested I try something else. I did not learn new skills there. I spent too much time talking to the patrons instead of selling drinks. I returned to being a patron and drinking away my loneliness from the absence of my Vince.

That is when I met this new guy at the bar. It started as a one-night stand, but we became friends when we relied on each other to talk about our significant others. He did not live with his wife, and I was engaged. He had horses and took me horseback riding. It was the first and last time I sat in a saddle! *The horse took off on me.* For the first time since meeting my Vince, I was in a friendly and sexual relationship with another man, despite my engagement.

I was guilty and could not hold cover over my engagement to Vince. My written letters to him slowed, and he could sense something was different when we had an opportunity to talk on the phone. I told him what went down, and it upset us both. *It should have ended there.*

The solution. Quit my job, give up my apartment, and move to South Korea to be with him. He sent me a one-way ticket to Seoul, and I left the country in June of 1991. *What was I thinking?*

My Second "I Do"

A NEW LIFE

*J*THOUGHT, WHAT A GREAT ADVENTURE THIS WOULD BE. I arrived safely in Seoul, South Korea, Walkman and a journal in hand. My transpacific flight was more than 10 hours long. I repeatedly listen to Clint Black's *Killin' Time* cassette to pass the time. A Korean gentleman sat next to me and did his best to teach me the Korean language symbols and corresponding sounds. *I didn't get it.* When we landed, I took a deep breath and realized the narrow lens of life as I knew just widened to reveal a larger world outside Arizona, outside the United States.

We were happy to see each other and be reunited. *Will Vince truly take care of me?* We stayed at a hotel that evening, and he was so gentle and warm. I believed he truly missed me and was proud to have me there with him. He even took the time to shave my legs. We did have our moments.

It was during the time of the Gulf War. I remember looking out of the hotel window, taking it all in. The sight of riot shield guards in front of government buildings was uneasy, but being with Vince, my 'babe,' felt like home to me. We were truly doing this.

Our apartment was not ready yet for us to move in. *What! Where am I going to stay?* We shared a twin bed in his dorm room with a roommate who slept in the other twin bed. It was a bit uncomfortable. *Adapt and overcome, he said.* Vince still worked nights, and his roommate worked days, and I adapted to both their work and sleep schedules.

There were moments in that dorm room when it was peacefully quiet, *shelter-istic*, and lonely. I got sick with the Korean Crud the first few weeks when I arrived. It was cold-like, and I had chest congestion for a couple of weeks. Our first Fourth of July together was an insight into his psyche. His memories of that holiday were unpleasant and evoked abandonment and anger. I listened in wonder and fear to his drunken recall when he said he was sent away to a facility for psychiatric counseling. It was a shocking awareness for me and a painful one for him.

He drank a lot, and I drank with him. I still could not keep up his pace. The soju, Korean alcohol, was not regulated, so you never really knew the proof. It made me sick most of the time. I didn't make the distinction at the time, but I think the heavy drinking was a way to numb his pain, as was mine. We were similar in that way.

MARRIAGE

We couldn't get married until Vince's birth certificate arrived in the mail. We scheduled our wedding, or rather, marriage contract signing date, something as ordinary as it was adventurous. We took a bus to Seoul and then caught a taxi. The first step was obtaining a marriage license then going to another office to get it approved. The taxi driver announced to us, "you married now!" One last stop to the American Embassy to register the marriage, and we were officially husband and wife. We had to do all this during business hours when he usually slept, so it was a big deal. *It made me feel important to him.*

In one afternoon, I went from being a tourist to a wife. Although, I was still a tourist because he wasn't an officer and was on an unaccompanied overseas tour without authorized dependents. *What was I doing here?* It was still necessary to renew my tourist visa. That was an adventure! With only $20 left in my pocket to pay the taxi driver, I was in a panic at the bus station. *I'm not going to be able to get back to the base.* Oh, what a day. Thankfully I made it back in one piece. We were celebrated at a routine party in the dorm with his work buddies. They toasted and played the song *The Rose* by Bette Midler for our first dance as man and wife. It was August 1991.

SONGTAN

We, at last, moved out of the dorm room and into our apartment in Songtan, an area in the northern end of Pyeongtaek, South Korea. There was a fish market and business district between our apartment and the Osan Air Base. Some of the businesses were bars, and some of the bars had women for men. *I just ignored that part.* It was within walking distance to the base and not so far that I could not carry our dirty clothes and his work battle dress uniforms (BDUs) to the base laundry facility for washing. *Those uniforms stunk!* I would try to take the basket on my head as the locals did. *It was easier.* We were also close enough to the base to hear the noises from the jets and close enough to other apartments that I could listen to the Korean couple arguing throughout the night outside the window of our apartment. *I couldn't understand what they were saying.*

Our apartment became a place for Vince and his buddies to hang out, have barbeques, and party. Drinking and drinking; there was much drinking to pass the off-duty time. Sometimes my husband would make pit stops at the bars to drink after work before coming home. I was often left alone in the apartment to wonder where he was and when he would return. *There were no cell phones in the 90s.* For them, there was work, party time, and rest. Most of the time, I had fun with Vince and his friends, but I found myself exhausted, left alone, and wanting something more.

HANDS OFF

We drank a lot! I was happy to move out of the dorm room and into our apartment. It was our first home together. We were taller than the refrigerator, and the heat ran under the floors. It was small but had enough space to hold his buddies when they came to have parties.

Once at a party where everyone had been drinking, Vince held me by the neck up against the wall. *I can't move.* His buddies jumped in to pull him away and stop him from choking me. *Why is he so angry?* However hard I try, I can't remember the reason for this outburst. His overreaction to whatever was said or done led to him trying to choke me. Once freed, I immediately ran out of the apartment; because flight was my go-to. I went upstairs to the top of our apartment building to catch my breath and clear my mind. *What the hell just happened?*

Alone and confused, I climbed onto the edge of the top wall and sat staring down at the ground from three stories. *I could jump to make it all stop.* If I jumped, would all this madness stop. I could not figure out what I got myself into. Vince was never threatening to me before this. Why now? I played out my falling to the ground from three stories and concluded that it could be final or only leave me injured. What would this news do to my mom, family, and friends? That was not worth the jump. I swung my legs back over safely to the rooftop and eventually returned to the apartment and went to bed. He gave an apology the next day, and we resumed life as nothing had happened. *I can still see the ground.*

On the other hand, there were times he showed compassion and concern. Like when I cut my hand trying to get the pit out of an avocado. It wouldn't stop bleeding, and I got a bit scared. I called Vince at work crying, and he immediately came to the rescue. When he arrived to find only a quarter-inch cut, he laughed but not until I had been calmed and cared for. I had to laugh too because it was not that bad, while it was more than a scrape. *Why did I panic?* I still have a scar on my left hand from the avocado incident.

WORK

I needed an occupation. *Why can't I relax?* I applied for and was offered a job on base as a recreational aide with Morale

Welfare and Recreation (MWR). It was nice to work again, even if it was part-time. I kept busy planning activities at the youth center office, processing paperwork, and as coach of the junior high and high school cheerleading squads. *This job was so much fun!* It gave me a much-needed outlet, was a distraction from boredom and was something I enjoyed. I was decreasing my stress level by measures. I liked that I was earning my own money too. I was honored to be selected as one of two coaches to be the All-Star Cheerleader Coaches, allowing me to supervise and coach the All-Star Cheerleaders on a trip to Japan. Leading a group of teen girls is a whole other kind of stress.

SAY WHAT!

In South Korea, I had my first experience living and working in a snowy climate. *There was snow everywhere!* In December 1991, I received a call at work after having some lab work done. I had missed a period and thought for sure something was wrong. It was the doctor's office. They called to tell me that I was pregnant. I said, "are you sure? Couldn't it be stress? I've been under a lot of stress." *I thought he couldn't have kids.* It wasn't stress; *we* were pregnant, something we did not plan. We were also apprehensive that I might miscarry again.

Georgia on My Mind

A NEW ASSIGNMENT

VINCE'S TOUR OF DUTY IN SOUTH KOREA WOULD END in February 1992. His new assignment was in Valdosta, Georgia, at Moody Air Force Base, with a report date in March. I came up with a plan. I could leave now and spend January and February with my family and friends in Arizona. When he returned stateside, he could meet me there. Then we could drive to Georgia together in the car I left in Arizona.

It was a great plan. *I needed a break.* I got much-needed rest and was able to go to the doctor at Luke Air Force Base. I stayed with my best friend, and when Vince arrived, he joined us. She was married and had a two-year-old little girl. When he returned to the old stomping ground, he began his usual drinking again. Now pregnant, I still couldn't keep up with him, nor did I want to. On one occasion, he went out with a buddy and didn't return until 4:00 p.m. the next day. *How could he do this here? It was embarrassing and shameful.* Now there were witnesses to my sadness and loneliness. I left him there to sleep it off and drove to my mom's house.

When my mom opened the door, I collapsed in her arms and started crying uncontrollably. I told her how it was in South Korea and what had happened the night before. *I was so ashamed.* My family and friends knew he drank too much and that I did the same when I was with him. *He wasn't a good influence.* I had new orders myself: to take care of the unborn baby. After my mini-breakdown, she pleaded all her arguments about why I should stay in Arizona and how men like him do not change. *She saw my hurt.* But I believed he would change; it would be different once the baby was born.

GEORGIA OR BUST!

We left the next day—*just me and him.* I left knowing how much my family and friends were against it, but I didn't listen. I knew they cared about me. I also knew my place was with him, especially now with a baby on the way. *How else was I going to take care of myself and a baby?* We arrived in Valdosta, Georgia, greeted by two of his buddies from Osan. They didn't skip a beat, and the party began again. The drinking continued.

Before we even moved into our place in Georgia, I found myself alone again in a hotel room, Moody Inn on base, waiting for him to come home after a night of partying. *Why won't he stop?* I was mourning my decision to follow him to Georgia.

I know it sounds like I was a codependent, no-life, couldn't keep myself occupied, pregnant woman who was new to town and didn't have anyone to talk to. I was. I felt sadness and shame about the situation I got myself into. *You didn't listen to your mom.* I had just left my family and friends, my support system, and there was no way I would call them for help now. They were right, and I was wrong, so I had to accept responsibility.

THE TRAILER

We moved into a trailer not too far from the base. We didn't have much furniture, just a bed and some kitchen items that I had from my apartment. Our trailer was immediately baptized by Vince with another night out partying. *Where was he?* This reality was hard to adjust to, especially staying alone in a new place. *Is there something wrong with me?* My priorities changed with the pregnancy, and I wanted his to change. I was furious that it did not.

I woke the following day to him lying on the living room floor. *When did he get home?* I woke him up, and clearly, he wanted to continue sleeping, but I persisted. I told him that if he could be out partying all night, he could get up and spend time with his wife. My words set him off into attack mode.

I don't know how long it lasted. I don't know how I went from standing upright and Vince lying on the carpet to me lying on the ground and Vince standing over me. He pulled me by my hair; my body followed in one direction and then another. I curled in the fetal position, not saying a word as my head and back were kicked several times by his foot. My mind froze. Time stood still. Only when it stopped did I start to tear up. I needed to get out of there. *Run!* I grabbed my purse and car keys and headed for the door. *He's not gonna let me go.* He blocked me and asked where I was going. I told him I was going to the hospital to ensure the baby was okay. He let me leave.

When I got to the base's front gate, the guards could see that I was tearful and upset. I needed to get to the hospital, and I needed to make sure my baby was okay. My focus was on those two things. *The baby.* The guard asked if I was okay to drive, and I implied yes by shaking my head. Still confused and worried about how my body felt around the lower back and the baby, I signed into the clinic. I explained what had just happened and wanted to ensure my baby was okay.

They quickly called my name and took me to a room where I had to repeat what had happened and that I wanted to get checked out to make sure the baby was okay. The nurse took my vitals and checked out where I said it hurt. They used an ultrasound machine, and everything checked out. I waited. Then, two military police officers came in and asked me to describe what happened. I repeated what had happened and told them that I had come to the clinic to ensure the baby was okay. The baby checked out, personnel filed a report, and I waited until they said I could leave. *Do I go back to the trailer?* I don't know exactly how it went down on his end, but they said he would be picked up and taken to his sergeant.

We both ended up back at our trailer with his assurance that it would not happen again. *Do I stay or go back to Arizona?* I didn't have a job or money to get back home, so I stayed. Apologies were given, and we went on as if nothing had happened again.

THE PREGNANCY

During the rest of the pregnancy, he worked nights. I worked part-time in the ticket and tours office during the day. My co-workers were wonderful, and I was relieved to converse with others. Another time he didn't come home, I was left without a car to get to work. I was more concerned with getting to work by 9:00 a.m. than with whom he may have been with all night. *Classic denial.* The base was not far from home, so I started to walk. I didn't hitchhike this time, and I was only five-six months pregnant. Unsolicited, a car stopped and offered me a ride. He was a stranger to me but knew Vince and was going to the base. I was very grateful. I don't understand why, but he was still gone when I got back home, and I found my Bible in the tub, scorched.

I became resentful and angry at him. *What was I even doing here if he was going out all the time?* Several more nights, I stayed up waiting for him to come home. I was so angry on one of those nights that I damaged a couple of his dragon statues. *That was my way of hurting him.* As if that would make things right. It didn't. What we were doing to each other was not conducive to a respectful, loving marriage. It was mind-boggling, and I did not know how to process my present circumstances.

I went to counseling alone. I needed help to figure out how to handle these repeated feelings of being defeated. One session included a non-stop crying fit. I was so upset about the Bible incident that I cried uncontrollably. My pregnant belly bounced rapidly, causing the counselor to excuse himself to get help to calm me. He told me he thought I was going to go into labor. This mix-up made me laugh-cry. He let out a nervous chuckle too.

It was getting close to my due date. That last weekend my husband stayed home—the whole weekend. It was strange for him to be around all weekend. I asked him why he did that. He said his first shirt thought it would be a good idea. So, oh, okay. We spent time together and got the car all cleaned out too. After a peaceful weekend, we went to bed Sunday evening, and around 3:40 a.m. the following day, I woke up to a wet bed. Did I pee on the bed? I shouted out "Babe!" towards the living room where he was sleeping, "I think my water just broke!"

He drove us to the base and told the front gate guards we needed to go to the hospital because we were having a baby. *Ironic.* We were checked in and settled in an exam room. He was with me during the 14-hour labor. That whole day there was news of a hurricane on its way to Florida. It was about 5:00 p.m., and Vince went to lay down for a bit of rest when the baby was ready to enter our world. The nurses woke him up and brought him back to the room just in time to see our baby born. *It's a girl!* The pregnancy was emotionally challenging, and the birth was a painful experience; it did some damage to the lower region of my body. Not one time did any medical staff mention the word *epidural.* I didn't even know a procedure like that existed. Andrew, a powerful and destructive Category 5 Atlantic hurricane that struck the Bahamas, Florida, and Louisiana in August 1992, did some damage. Sixty-five people died as a result. My daughter's life had just begun; my life finally felt whole.

My hospital stay was four days. On the last day —a Thursday— the nurse went over discharge instructions with me; she waited until I was alone. She also gently and kindly asked me if I felt safe going home. *How did they know?* The military police, military hospital, and military counseling knew about our tumultuous marriage. It would be different now, with a baby at home. I did feel safe. I told her so. I let her know that my in-laws would arrive the next day and stay for ten days. I got my discharge papers, and we brought our baby home to the trailer.

My in-laws were so helpful as I was overwhelmed with the uncertainty of my marriage, exhausted from the emotional struggles, and nervous about being a first-time mom. My memories of their visit are the home cooking, washer and dryer, and baby's first bath by her dad. As soon as they drove away to return to Illinois, I felt the apprehension rising again.

NOT AGAIN

As it turns out, it did not make a difference when the baby arrived. Near the end of October, there was another fight. Since he had been going out again, I thought I would take a turn. *I'll show him I can do it too.* He was not down for that. We had been arguing, and as I attempted to leave, my head got in the way of a swinging door. *Oh, dang, that hurt.* I barely got out and ran to the neighbor's house to ask them to call the police. She said they did and asked why we were always fighting. With him being so angry, I felt I needed to get back into the trailer to stay with the baby. There was no going out for me that night. *I guess it was still his turn.*

The next day we received notice of eviction. We needed to find a new place to live. He found one with a roommate, and the baby and I flew to Arizona. He let me go. It wasn't a break-up as much as a break that I needed. To avoid emotional explanations, I called it the baby tour. *I needed to be with my family.* After a visit to Arizona, we flew to Nashville, Tennessee. There, his parents picked us up to spend time with them. *It was their turn.* Vince would then drive up from Georgia at Thanksgiving, and we would go home as a family and start over in a new place.

THE APARTMENT

We settled into a new apartment further from the base and closer to the town of Valdosta. I stayed home with the baby, and he worked nights, still. It was on the second floor, and I remember carrying Vanessa in one hand and the groceries in the other, up and down the stairs a few times to get them all in. *I can do this.* I managed as best I could. Adapt and overcome, right.

The nights of him not coming home began again. *Why am I even here?* It was the same unchanged routine—the same need to party for him and the same kind of loneliness for me. I was the unhappy one. Our marriage was in complete disarray. It would be a couple of good days at the beginning of the week, and then the weekends would come knocking. On the good days, it was nice. His behavior on weekends was why I questioned the commitment as a married couple and now as parents.

By January 1993, we made plans for me and the baby to leave. We would move to Arizona once we received our tax return. Again, it wasn't a break-up as much as it was a much-needed break. So, Vanessa and I made our way across Interstate-10 to Arizona by car, by ourselves. He let us go.

Back Home

MOM'S COUCH

WE DROVE ACROSS INTERSTATE-10 BACK TO MY hometown of Phoenix, Arizona. Vanessa was a pleasant passenger, and I held tightly onto her when we would stop for gas or food. It took three days of driving to get there. *I was determined to get home safely.* When we stopped for the night, I found the closest Mexican restaurant to have dinner, bringing me closer and closer to the taste of home. The spices were different along the way, and I was looking for the taste of the Southwest. I needed to refill my cup with family, friends, familiarity, culture, and peace. If I was going to be alone and feel alone while raising my baby, I might as well do it on my own with family by my side.

We stayed with my mom on her couch. It was sad and heartbreaking that Vince and I were a separated family. It could be a thousand miles or no distance, which wouldn't make any difference. I was relieved to be home and no longer be directly affected by his idea of marriage and fatherhood. It was time to move forward and take care of Vanessa and me. *I gotta get a job.*

When I left Arizona, the job skills I had to offer were the same general job skills I had when I returned. I relied upon my mad secretarial talent and charm and soon landed a job where my aunt, sister, best friend, and two cousins worked. A family friend had a home daycare, so I left Vanessa in her care while working 40 hours a week. We were settling in and developed a routine. My cup was half happy and half sad, which was better than runneth over with sadness.

In May, Vince flew in from Georgia over the Memorial Day weekend to visit us and participate in Vanessa's baptism. I had asked my sister and her ex-husband to be Nina and Nino. It wasn't difficult; they only needed to show up at Luke Air Force base and participate. There was strife before the baptismal date about whether they would show up because Vince would be there. We waited. *They're not coming.* I am grateful that Lisa, Vanessa's babysitter, and her husband were there to step in. My sister and her ex-husband's refusal to attend would later be used against me by Vince to "prove" that my family didn't care about me and that he did. *I started to believe him.*

This situation left the door open to talk about getting back together. I agreed. When Vince returned to Georgia, I let him take Vanessa with him. I gave two weeks' notice to work and then immediately drove straight back to Georgia to give our marriage another try. My mom objected to this plan, and I found myself on my best friend's couch those last two weeks. It was stressful, and I believe I drank every night after work before hitting the road. My leaving, again, was against my families' better judgment. But he promised me things would be different. *He promised.* My family saw something more clearly about Vince than I would allow myself to see. "Men like that never change," my mom would say. I left anyway. It took me two days this time. Vanessa was not yet one, and in those two weeks, she forgot who I was for a hot minute when I returned. That moment broke my heart. Thankfully, this absence of mind was short-lived.

ANOTHER APARTMENT

Vince picked out a lovely two-bedroom, bi-level apartment for us to move into. It was the summer of 1993 when we got back together. I wanted us to be a family. We made a trip to SeaWorld in Orlando, Florida together. He was so good at giving me little nuggets of hope. *He was reeling me in again.* It felt like things would work out this time.

It wasn't long before history began repeating itself. This dysfunctional relationship is how life was ever since the pregnancy and arrival of our baby. We would go in and out of sync, and our fondness for each other would grow and then fade. We started to take turns going out. I had less than a handful of friends and had gone out with them or on my own to have "my turn." One of those nights, we got a babysitter and went out together to a bar. He wanted to see if any guys knew me, for if they did, he would kick their ass. *I felt like a paraded possession.* This night out was an unpleasant experience.

I needed an occupation. I started a part-time job at the Main Street Program for the City of Valdosta. My hours were

8:00 a.m. to noon. This schedule became "my time" and offered me an outlet for the insanity at home. I left Vanessa at home with Vince while I worked, and I swear they slept most of the time. I blame him for her eventually becoming a night owl.

I had an odd experience at work one morning. The city was planning a parade. Mind you; I was not well-studied in the Civil War, slavery, and the formation of the KKK. I knew Valdosta was the location for the movie *Fried Green Tomatoes*, but I didn't realize that it was also home to a KKK group. One of their leaders came into the office to look at the parade route map. *Oh my god, did he just say...* I overheard my boss talking to him. A definitive freeze moment for this non-European-American indeed. After he left, I asked my boss about it. With all the confidence and casualness in the world, she said yes, they have the right to participate in the parade (heavy Georgia accent included). I had only heard about this organization and did not realize it was still a thing. It was.

ROLLERCOASTER

No matter how much Vince and I tried, our marriage was on the rocks again. This time, it was an up against the wall fight and an in-your-face screaming match that he would end with a spat in my face. I think I kicked the garbage basket down to the floor too. There was no choking, kicking, or pulling of the hair, just a push and press against the wall. I physically, emotionally, and irrationally broke down and retreated upstairs to Vanessa's bedroom. I took comfort on the floor, curled into the fetal position, and prepared for a complete meltdown cry-fest. *I can't believe I came back to Georgia. Why did I come back?* This woman-girl could not make sense of her life, marriage, or future. I wailed it out for more than 20 minutes and had more disbelief in me, but I exhausted myself. I think this crying episode scared Vince. I remember him checking in on me a few times. As much as I felt confused and hopeless, I am sure he did not know what to make of it. It was a way to flush all the overflowing ugly feelings. I had a limit, and I had reached it that day. Then it was on to prepare myself to adapt and overcome once again. *I was too ashamed to go back home now.*

My boss, Robin, knew an attorney who would be willing to help me file for divorce. I could not do life with him anymore. Marital promises were broken, and it was time to set ourselves free. I brought the divorce papers home for him to look through. He did. He also convinced me not to file and that things would be different.

The future would bring another pregnancy into the marriage. *What in the world.* How could I bring another child into this unhappy, dysfunctional, unbalanced marriage in this God-given world? Less than two months ago, I brought home divorce papers. I could not. I was contemplating an abortion again. I looked at options and found a place in a nearby city. I needed money to do this, so I called my mom. We talked it through, and in the end, my mom did not have 300 dollars to send me for the procedure. She was still a single mother supporting my brother and a devout Catholic. I didn't have the money. I'm not even sure I made it onto the checking account. This time, the circumstances decided for me. I did not have the means to have a selective abortion. Therefore, "Babe, I'm pregnant!" His reply, "That baby better be mine." *Really?* This recrimination would go on throughout the pregnancy.

THE HOUSE

After a few months of pregnancy, it was time to go back to Arizona for a visit. My cup was on the low end, and it needed filling again by my family. I took another baby tour with Vanessa as baby number two grew in my belly. I can only imagine what my life looked like from their view; I could have been a walking advertisement for a Lifetime movie. I knew they all wanted what was best for me and that they did care about me. Heck, I could see them struggling in their way as well. I would tell myself they had to work and children of their own to care for, which is why they couldn't afford to visit me. It was always more efficient for me to visit them and see many than any one of them to visit only me. This logic was true. It was also true that none of my family or friends were fond of Vince; no matter how much I loved him, they did not. *I was "in love" with him.*

When we returned to Valdosta, it was another new place, in a new city in Berrien County. Vince had rented a house in Nashville, Georgia, a town 16 miles away from the air force base and even further from the city of Valdosta. *Isolation?* It immediately felt like isolation.

At seven months pregnant, we settled down and made another fresh start on our marriage with a 20-month-old and a new baby on the way. We had a scheduled date set for delivery to avoid broken water surprises, except for the baby's gender.

My mother-in-law and Vince's brother drove from Illinois to Georgia to be there for the birth. I welcomed her presence—especially the morning of the delivery. Vince's brother stayed home with Vanessa, and then we were off to have a baby in the early morning. This time it was off base at South Georgia Medical Center. They gave me something called an *enema* as preparation before the delivery, unlike the hospital on base. But, okay. *What in the world!* It was an awful experience. I never, ever want to experience that again. Then, they asked if I was having an epidural. *No one mentioned that was an option.* I wasn't sure what an epidural was. I told them that no one had talked to me about that. So, they moved on.

Meme (Vince's mom) took over about 9:00 a.m. so Vince could take a break early in the labor process. Based on the last time, we figured labor would take a while. So, he went to the cafeteria for a snack, and sure enough, our baby was ready to enter the world. *I have to puuuuuuush!* The doctor returned to the room—and so did Vince from the cafeteria—because the baby was coming.

He made it back on time, and three pushes later, our second baby arrived. "It's a girl!" said the doctor. An episiotomy followed the delivery of a healthy baby girl. They discharged me and our baby, Victoria, the next day.

Illinois Bound

THE IN-LAWS' HOUSE

SOON AFTER VICTORIA'S ARRIVAL, VINCE GOT HIS RANK advancement results back and learned that his military career would end within one year. *He should have been studying instead of drinking all the time.* He was not eligible for reenlisting after the ten-year mark. That left us a year to prepare for civilian life. I came up with a plan! *I want to go home.* The kids and I would move now, and I would get a job and a place to live so there would be no gap in income or housing upon his discharge. Me: Let's move to Arizona. Him: Let's move to Illinois. We debated and discussed the cost and benefits of both. Arizona was far away, and to start with, I would have to stay with my mom. She was still taking care of my little brother, and I had two little kids now. The couch would not do this time. Illinois was a bit closer, and his parents had a spare room that we could use until I saved enough money to move out. We chose Illinois.

In September 1994, the girls and I packed up and drove to Illinois. *He let us go.* Victoria was a little over two months, and

Vanessa was two years old. I was still breastfeeding Victoria, which made feeding a little easier while traveling, but I had to stop more. Over one long day, we made it to Joppa safely. It was nice and peaceful at his parent's house. As quiet as an Italian family could be. I sure did not feel alone, but I felt very welcomed. The food was delicious, and being around his family filled the void of me missing mine.

October 31st was my first day on the job at an insurance company inside Peoples Bank in Paducah, Kentucky. I set up daycare for the girls at Polliwog Place in Metropolis, which was on the way to work in Paducah. I had to leave Joppa by 7:15 a.m. to drop the girls off at daycare and then make it across the Ohio River and report to work by 8:00 a.m.

Vince drove from Georgia to Illinois to be with us at Thanksgiving and Christmas, but he still had to work and finish his last year. In mid-January, I took Vanessa to the hospital due to an ear infection that caused a high temperature for over a week. She required IV antibiotics and fluids to bring down her fever before they could perform an ear tube procedure. My mother-in-law kept Victoria while I stayed with Vanessa in the hospital for five days. A co-worker came by to check on us and stayed with Vanessa for a little bit to give me a break. Little miss Vanessa had already had a low iron issue when we first arrived in Illinois that came close to needing a blood transfusion. *This child had me worried. I should have breastfed her.* With iron drops, her numbers began to rise again. Although Vince's mom was very helpful, I felt like I was already practicing for single-mother life.

MY OWN PLACE

By February 1995, I had saved enough money while staying with Vince's parents to move into a place at Devondale Apartments, an affordable housing community in Metropolis. A place to call my very own. This place was *my* apartment. Mine. A simple, very nice two-bedroom space that was clear of any awful memories.

Three other women were there in the next-door apartment and, the two above, raising their kids as single mothers, Patty, Valerie, and Becky. Another very cool young lady lived there, Erica, whom I would talk to now and then. Erica and I didn't know this at the time, but we would become more connected with each other in the future.

My girls and I lived in a peaceful environment for the next four months. I was free of any fear of abandonment or altercation in my own space. During this time, I learned some new skills: time management in getting my two babies and me ready for daycare and work, money management in paying my bills again, creative fun in keeping me and the girls occupied while waiting for their father to join us. I also learned that I could take care of myself and my girls independently. *He better not pull any of that funky business when he gets here.* I didn't have to take crap from anyone anymore.

My year was closing in, and he would be here soon. *Is this anxiety? Push it down, girl.* I began to feel more and more unsettled as the date got closer to his honorable discharge from the military.

WELCOME HOME

In June 1995, we celebrated his return with a welcome home party and a one-year birthday party for Victoria. It was at the Joppa Community Center with family and friends. It turned out very nice. Later, a co-worker would share with me her observation that there was a disconnect between Vince and me and was concerned. *Everything is fine.*

MY 30ᵀᴴ BIRTHDAY

The following month, "You lazy bitch," is what my husband gifted me on my 30th Birthday. I woke up early with the girls and made us pancakes. We saved some pancake batter for Vince for when he woke up. I was busy with the girls, and he wanted me to cook him some pancakes. I suggested that he could make some with the batter we saved for him. My suggestion led to an argument that caused us to be at odds. *Oh my, it's starting again.* And I fell for it. We had plans to go out together that evening. It would have been a good opportunity for me to meet more people. Instead, he went alone and stayed out until the following day.

REUNION TIME

About 6:30 a.m., he makes it back home. He had been drinking. Vanessa was with me, and Victoria stayed the night with my mother-in-law. I unlocked the door to let him in and asked the typical questions a wife would ask when her husband was out all night. I headed back to my bed where Vanessa and I were sleeping, and the arguing started. *I can't believe you are doing this to me again.* I just wanted to go back to sleep with

Vanessa, and I didn't want him in the room. I tried to shut and lock the door, but that didn't stop him. I shouted, "Get out! Leave me alone!" I will never forget his response, "I can beat the shit out of you, and no one would come; you can't do anything about it!" I told him I would call the police if he did not get out of the room. *If you can't handle an immediate threat, call the police.* He wouldn't get out, so I called the local police department. He would always be bigger and stronger than me, and I would never be able to defend myself against him. Never. As author Malcolm Gladwell would say, for me, this incident was the moment of clarity, my "tipping point."

The police arrived. I explained the situation, telling the officers that I didn't feel safe with him there. He was drunk, and he threatened to "beat the shit out of me" in front of my child, and I wanted him to leave. I will never forget their response; they said they could not make him leave because he was my husband. *Are you kidding me!* I pleaded that this was my apartment, my name was on the lease, and I paid the rent. I want him out!. Instead, the officers would allow him to stay. *This is nuts!* It was mindboggling that this was the response I got from the police. *"Serve and protect" my ass!* I did not know how to react to their response at that moment. Survival mode kicked in, and I asked if they could stick around long enough for me to get some items for my daughter and me so that we could leave. They did. And I left. I drove to his mom's house, let myself in, and slept in his brother's room until folks there woke up. I let his parents know what had happened and that I was done.

NO MORE

I did not want him in my apartment. I did not want to talk to him. I did not want anything to do with him anymore. *I am not doing this anymore!* When I returned later that day, I let him know this. I wanted him out, and the split would be final this time. No more separations. No more chances. No more apologies would do—none. *I love you, I love you so much, but I can't do this anymore.* I decided I was no longer "in love" with him, and my emotional detachment kicked in. No amount of desire would ever change our circumstances. He had no control over his drinking, and I had no control over him. I challenged him repeatedly to be a husband to me as he had promised and to be the father I imagined for my girls. I held on for four years for us to become a family unit. It was not going to happen now or anytime in the future. The only thing I had control over was eliminating the threat to my girls and me. I would distance myself from the anger, abuse, deceit, and infidelity and give up on this love story. Something deep in my soul clicked, and I was on the road to divorce city again. *This final decision broke my heart and soul.* I was broken.

TKO Love

FIGHT, FLIGHT, AND FREEZE; THAT IS HOW MARRIED LIFE was. I did not want that anymore. In total, we were married for five years. We lived in the same home for only 22 months due to all the separations and baby tours. My mind was ready to move on, but I was heartbroken and damaged. But before I left this time, I needed to make it final so that I could move on. Let's get this taken care of legally to move on.

He made the first move. I was served with divorce papers that contained the most ridiculous and outrageous demands. *He wants full custody!* He and his attorneys had to be delusional. The girls were three and one; he wanted full child custody and objected to me moving to Arizona with the girls! *He hadn't opposed before.* It was a preemptive strike to prevent me from moving back home and an attack on me, my character, and my future with the girls. I had no defense fund, no defense team, no defense strategy. I thought we would divorce, pack up my car, hook up a trailer with our possessions, and drive back to Arizona. And that he would let me go. He had let me go before—many times. I completely did not understand his objection.

The letter from his attorney indicated I was to sign and return the documents by a specific date. My salary paid enough for basics needs, but it wasn't enough for many extras, especially attorney's fees. I didn't have a lawyer to respond to the ridiculous petition and feared the outcome if I didn't do something. *What am I gonna do?*

A LITTLE HELP

Someone from the bank building where I worked told me about an agency that helped with legal services. I applied for legal assistance with the Land of Lincoln Legal Aid and desperately awaited a response. I pleaded my case with the written word pouring my heart out about the current circumstances. I felt like I had won the lottery when I received notice of approval for a local attorney to represent my girls and me.

Anthony Lloyd represented me, and he and his staff, Nikita and Verna, would become my new heroes. *Fear and abandonment paralyzed me.* I was merely their boss's client, but they were three more people added to the few I knew in this town. A town I was trying to escape from. They were sweet angels and showed the utmost professional kindness each time I had a meeting with Mr. Lloyd.

SMALL TOWN

This small town felt even smaller to me. I didn't know its history but knew one of its main attractions was a statue of Superman in the town square, and I needed a hero. In 1972, the Illinois State Legislature declared Metropolis, IL, the "Hometown of Superman." Other cool things about this town were the burial site of a convicted murderer, the "Birdman of Alcatraz," and Fort Massac State Park, the location of an annual reenactment of late-1700s life on the frontier with mock battles and food from the era. It was also home to Curt Jones, Dippin' Dots ice cream creator, and Christopher Jackson, who played George Washington in *Hamilton's* Broadway play.

The not-so-cool thing about a small town is its gossip channels, perceived and real. Vince was a local, and I wasn't. More people knew him than they did me, a thought that fed my vulnerability and insecurity. They all knew my husband was cheating on me and whom he was sleeping with. Sounds paranoid, but that is what it felt like to me until my attorney said something in one of our conversations: "most people have their own lives to worry about; they are not concerned with yours." *Blunt, but oh so true.* What Vince was doing and how unfair the situation felt to me kept my mind trapped. I had been the girls' primary caretaker, and he, as usual, was running around the town. This assertion was a convincing piece of wisdom from my attorney that knocked me down a notch and helped me move forward emotionally, even if by a little. I had to adapt and overcome small-town gossiping, focusing only on the goal of divorce and returning to my hometown in Arizona.

PATIENCE

I would meet with my attorney several more times over the next year. There were delays and postponements, and

I became more anxious, lonelier, and sadder. One of the postponements was due to my attorney becoming ill and hospitalized. He needed a donor's liver. I visited him in the hospital and wanted to make sure he would be okay. *That's what you do, right.* His health was rightly prioritized over his work, although he continued to work whenever possible.

PETITIONER

It must have been a bluff from Vince's attorneys when they sent me those papers. We were the party to file petitions to the court first, making me the petitioner and him the defendant. My petition included a desire for me to have full custody of the girls and to be able to move back to my hometown in Arizona. I was honest with my attorney and gave him the information to support our case. It took nearly a year to get an answer. During this time, my employer, the insurance company, laid me off. *It was nice to be home with my girls.* I hoped that this would free me up to move to Arizona. I knew more jobs were available in a larger city than in a small town. And honestly, I just wanted to go home, be home, and make a home for my girls and me.

THE HEARING

The court finally set a hearing date before the presiding circuit judge, the Honorable Judge Foster. The one judge assigned to Massac County, Illinois, First Judicial Circuit Court. He heard our cases; the lawyers presented their clients' demands, asked questions, and questioned our characters. My attorney had to quiet me when I interrupted testimony to protest that "He's not telling the truth!" It's up to the judge to discern the truth and determine what is in the children's best interest. But you're supposed to tell the truth when you testify in court! I was shocked to learn otherwise. My truth explained why I should have custody of the girls and why it was best for me to relocate. His truth stated why he should get custody of the girls and petitioned for them to stay. The court proceeding was such a miserable experience. Getting a divorce with no kids involved is so much easier; trust me, I know.

SHOCK

I was shocked once again when the judge handed down his decision to deny my *"Petition to Remove the Minor Children from the State of Illinois to the State of Arizona."* I got the good news/bad news over the phone. The good news was that the girls would be in my care full-time, granting visitation for him. This decision broke my heart, spirit, and mind. Not the visitation part, since that was never in question; I didn't want to prevent that. The age of the girls, the distance between state lines, and the ability of either one of us to facilitate long-distance visitation were at issue. It made sense (not at the time), but that did not change the level of devastation and disappointment when I got that phone call. If those three single-mother neighbors of mine were home, they would have heard a deep, soul-crushing, bone-chilling murderous scream from my apartment that day as I fell to the floor and died a little. That woman-girl was lost, and with a new layer of heartache added to her inner survival child. This situation was DB material big time.

PLANNING TO ESCAPE

I collected myself and called my mom with the news. We began planning my escape home. Our rational minds walked through the scenarios which didn't look good. What would happen if the girls and I just left? Vince would take the court order to the local sheriff's office, and they would contact the Maricopa County Sheriff's Office. This action would likely lead to my arrest for defying a court order, and the kids would be taken away by strangers and transported back to Illinois. I would land in jail, probably lose custody of the girls, and have a criminal record. *That's what could happen.* This potential scenario would be traumatic for the girls, and I would not want to leave them here without a mother. I've lived the story of an absent parent, and it didn't turn out well. I was too afraid of the consequences. I would need to adapt and overcome as this was my only choice. I would stay and make the best life possible for my girls and me.

A GLORIOUS SISTERHOOD

A crazy good thing came out of my frequent trips to the courthouse for divorce proceedings for over a year. A kind lady at the County Clerk's Office invited me to a Zeta Zeta Sorority rush party. It's a community service organization that is part of "Beta Sigma Phi International for the best friends of your life!." It would be an excellent way to meet people and become involved. I prepared for this rush party with an open mind and fight mode if needed. I had only heard of college sororities, not community service sororities that offered a pledge of support and sisterhood. The house was in a beautiful, rich-looking neighborhood. I had never been in a home as nice as the one I went to that night. Just as lovely were the ladies. They invited me back to become a member. I accepted and have been a member since 1996.

OTHER GOOD NEWS

I was called back to my former job and returned to full-time work. In a short time, I studied for and tested successfully as a licensed insurance agent, general lines. *I never practiced insurance.* I stayed working as a receptionist for several months and had begun to plant seeds of a new life in a small town.

DUNG BAG

The divorce was not the worst thing that happened between Vince and me. It was the history of us that caused triggers. I also felt like a failure as a wife and a mom. I knew it had to end, though. Seeing him move on so quickly was the most painful to absorb. Losing connection with his family was heartbreaking too. I was going at it alone for a while. Adapting and overcoming had become exhausting. There was no other choice but to dust off and take two steps forward, even if it meant one step backward from time to time.

Now What

GOOD INTENTIONS

WHO ENTERS THE MARITAL STATE WITH A TERM LIMIT in mind? I didn't the first time or the second time. It was my second divorce, so what was wrong with me? I was 0-2 in the "I do" department and am now a single mother with two young children. It was not my intention to quit my job in Arizona, hop on a plane to a foreign country, get married to a man I've known for less than a year, have a child, and then another child, only to divorce and be ordered to stay in a town where I didn't know anyone. I was fully committed to Vince, and I adored him; I would have followed him anywhere. I left my home to become a military wife and support him in his military career. The afterward cost-benefit analysis would prove a loss in the love-life column and an exceedingly plus in the lives-loved column, namely my girls. The proclamation of love between Vince and me was not enough. Parts of me died each time indifference replaced love.

BORN AGAIN

I can't say I ever was a devout catholic. I can say that my mom and most of our family were catholic. Ironically, my sister Joanne was the only one of us to make Confirmation. I started classes at St. Augustine Roman Catholic Church near our home in West Phoenix but never finished. At this turning point in my life, I felt lost and needed some finding. So, I leaned on my catholic roots and went to the local catholic church, St. Rose of Lima.

I made an inquiry to the pastor about making my first Holy Communion and Confirmation. Honest to goodness, he told me he had to get back with me. Besides feeling confused and rejected, it felt like a jab from the church spire. I respected Father Joe; he baptized my daughter, Victoria, when she was about four months old at this very same church. *And he had to get back with me?*

He contacted me to let me know I could pursue the Confirmation process. I began retaking classes at age 30 with the help of a teenage girl who needed service hours. She watched the girls for me while I went to classes. A very nice lady sponsored me; she would accompany me to Belleville, Illinois, to gain the blessing of Confirmation from Bishop Wilton Gregory. This bishop has since been elevated to the rank of cardinal by Pope Francis in November of 2020 and is the first African American cardinal. *That makes me feel kind of special.*

In one of my sessions with Father Joe, I asked him what God would think of my getting a divorce. His reply came in the form of a question: Would God want you to stay in the marital circumstances you were in? I said, "No!" adamantly. From then on, I considered myself a born-again human being and did not feel the curse of a divorce, or two, upon me.

THE OTHER WOMAN

During the one-year divorce proceedings, I had to accept my husband taking our girls to stay overnight with him at the house where he was living off and on with a woman. *Knowing this made me sick.* Her home was on 10th Street, the main road I drove on to get to daycare and work. One such morning I spotted his car parked at her house. I had been in denial in the past, but seeing it myself took the heartbreak to a new level. I screamed inside my car as if the sheer volume of my vocals would erase the pain of that sight. It didn't. Instead, I got a bout of laryngitis and lost my voice for about three weeks, no other medical reason but for stress and maybe for screaming.

COUNSELING

I felt overwhelmed and sought counseling to process the post-divorce emotions that kept creeping up and choking me. *My hurt would not go away.* I saved money to go to one counseling session at a large Baptist church in Paducah, Kentucky. I used my hour to complain about my ex-husband and what I thought he should and should not be doing. My world had gotten smaller with this divorce, and the radius of distrust more considerable. Being stuck in Illinois made it more difficult for me emotionally. It was bearable before his military discharge, but now he was right in front of me. If I didn't see what he was doing, I would hear about it. *People want to tell you that they saw him and what he was doing.* Party life. It wasn't fair. He had his mom to help him, and I had only me. Child support was minuscule, and daycare fees were a large portion of my take-home pay. This period was an emotionally exhausting and financially struggling time for me.

The fee for that counseling was worth every dollar. Here is a snippet from that session:

Preacher: When you get to heaven and stand before God, will Vince be standing there next to you telling God all about you?

Me: (shocked) Absolutely not!

Preacher: When Vince gets to heaven and stands before God, will you be standing there next to him telling God all about him?

Me: (stumped)... Nope... (deep breath).

Dang, the preacher put me in my place. The point was well-received, and it would begin the process of letting him go and grabbing on to me. I would often rely on this snippet about what others said or did. I needed that counsel. Overall, the idea of a nuclear family with Vince was not to be. It still hurt, and the concern for what he would do with his personal life began only to be limited to where it concerned our girls. I put the loss in the DB.

HOLIDAYS AND SUCH

I cried and fell to the floor after shutting the door when he would pick up the girls for their visitation. I experienced the odd and even years of holidays, separate birthday celebrations, and the plans that fell on and off designated visitation weekends. Initially, an adjustment period chipped away at my heart and mind, but it leveled out. I found relief knowing that Vince either lived with or took the girls to his mom's house for his visitations. I turned visitation time into "me time." I just wanted them to be safe and happy. They were.

I had the kindest co-workers who invited me to spend Thanksgiving and Christmas with their families. I would spend the New Year at home with my girls. After a divorce, sharing children means alternating them on special occasions; therefore, celebrating with your children becomes more important than the actual holiday or celebration. This realization was a harsh lesson, and it was better to learn it sooner than later.

Days after the divorce was final, I went to my first sorority meeting. It was my time to socialize with other women twice a month and volunteer in community activities. I met many friendly people throughout my sorority membership, and some were not as friendly.

STUCK

I'm a failure. That was my self-talk. It would take a while before I dug myself out of this internal wound. I am stuck in this place (more self-talk). Survival mode took over, and there was no time to heal the wounds. They would remain untreated for years.

ACCEPTANCE

I decided that I wasn't going anywhere for a while. *The judge decided this for me.* This small town was now my new home.

I had to share my girls with their dad and move the post-divorce scale from the side of bitterness to the side of something not so bitter. It was hard and took time. I had to become emotionally detached from Vince to succeed for the girls' sake. When it came to their dad, whatever I did, would do, or had to suck up, would be for my girls. I never wanted to plant my history with their dad on them, and they needed to have a relationship with him; if I couldn't have the best part of him, I wished it upon my girls.

DATES AND ONE NIGHTS

Every other weekend I would have time to go out and let loose. I met some guys while being out with friends, and they set me up on a few dates. I didn't mind the dates. It was an opportunity to feed my social desires and feed off a steak dinner. That's right; the food was more important than the connection! *The emotional detachment was becoming easier and easier.* A steak dinner could feed me and provide enough leftovers for another meal at home.

I met other needs with one-nighters or two in some cases. Other times would be interview-type conversations that did not lead anywhere. Some guys were more curious about my past with Vince than about me. That soon got old. I only wanted human connections and fun times that didn't extend past my "me time" weekends. *No commitments from me.*

Going out with the girls was fun and filled my need for friendship connections. I didn't feel so alone, and I began to see familiar faces. This was a nice time and filled a void when I didn't have my kids.

CRITICAL THINKING

I'll admit this one. I was critical and was determined to strike first. I was not interested in a love connection. It was war—a war against men. *I'll show you not to mess with me.* As much as I appreciated the meals and conversations, I looked for a reason not to grant a second date. If he smoked, he was gone; if a man sent me two dozen red roses too soon, he was gone; if we didn't click, he was gone; and, no, I do not want to date your ex-husband, please. *Did a woman really ask me that?* Most of all, I would not invest any time or energy to change a person. I would be judge, jury, and executioner.

I would dedicate myself to my girls. They would be my priority. They couldn't hurt me, and I could love them fully for as long as I breathed. I would work to support them and be present in their lives. Even more important was to protect them. *I must protect them.* I never wanted what had happened to me to ever happen to them. That became my mindset.

OFF TRACK

In early 1997, I got a little off track when I was laid off again from the insurance company. I was eligible for unemployment benefits for six months. I saw this as a change of circumstances and wanted to petition the court to allow me and the girls to move back to Arizona. Even though I began to settle in, I still felt stuck in Illinois.

I was assigned a new attorney, and we proceeded with the petition and other outstanding issues, mostly about medical bills and child support. I searched for jobs in Illinois and Arizona unsuccessfully. The circumstances were not in my favor. We received the same decision as before, but we did settle up some back child support and a portion of severance pay from the military. That was a little win because we keep score, right?

I enjoyed the opportunity to be home with my girls and regroup. We had a great time doing fun activities that didn't cost much money. It became stressful for me to wait for the court decision, and it was getting close to the end of unemployment benefits. I couldn't seem to find a job and was getting worried. My mom sent money to help during the seventh month of being unemployed, and I qualified for cash assistance and food stamps. It was time for a piece of luck to drop out of the sky.

WHO YOU KNOW

Living in a small town where folks "know" each other had its advantages. My new attorney was dating the brother of a local college advisor. The latter "knew" of a job opening at a local river transportation company and happened to drop my name for this job at a family gathering. The job was part-time and would pay enough for rent, utilities, gas, and basics. The government helped with childcare costs; I received a rent subsidy from a housing program, the Illinois Medicaid covered medical assistance for my girls and we received food stamps. I don't know how I would have made it without these social safety net programs. I felt the application process for these programs was humiliating. Although the public aid office personnel did not make me feel inferior, being in need made me feel less. I needed to be able to work and have medical care for my children. *I gotta do this for the girls.* It was worth any humiliation I felt, and the aid was temporary.

YOU'RE HIRED

The job interview went so well that the man who interviewed me used my contact information to call me off-hours. *Men are freakin' dogs!* He liked me, and it wasn't only for my mad office skills. I did muster up a friendly personality, so I don't blame him too much. *But still.* It was one of those nights out with the girls, and I mentioned to him where we would be. Long story short, he showed up, we had some beers, we left, we were in my car, and we kissed. *Ugh! Not happening.* That was it. He left, and I went home. I got the job. He was my boss for over three years. We ignored that night and never went down that road again.

I started part-time in October of 1997 and by February of 1998 was offered a full-time job with benefits! I was so proud to contact the public aid office to notify them of my full-time job status. *Yes! I don't need your help anymore but thank you.* Medical insurance for the girls fell upon their dad, but his employment situation did not allow it. Thankfully, the girls continued to be covered by Medicaid. Other programs ended since they were income-based. *And I now had a salary income!* I will always support and be grateful for the social safety net programs made available to my girls and me by the state of Illinois.

FLEXIBILITY

Vince and I had settled into a post-divorce, post-second petition to leave routine. We put aside hurt feelings for the sake of our children, and cooperation had elevated to meet the needs of both parties; rather, three parties: Vince, his mom, and I. *Thank goodness for Meme.* After a few bumps in the road, we started working outside the terms of visitation and achieved a flexible balance for the sake of our girls. *It was hard for me to accept help.* This process was challenging emotionally, but we did it.

When couples with children are divorcing, emotions run high before, during, and after the proceedings, especially when a case involves accusations of abuse and infidelity. I wanted to move home to be with my family, and he wanted his girls to stay. In the end, we each got what was most important to us. I wanted full custody of the girls more than I wanted to move home. He wanted the girls to stay so he could have a relationship with them. And that's how it was.

SECOND THOUGHTS

In the spring of 1998, two years after the divorce was final, I reached a tipping point. *Did I do the right thing?* Should I have tried one more time? Post-divorce, life was still lonely, and the hurt from the loss remained. I left him to keep my children from growing up in an unhealthy environment. It was the right thing to do. Why did I have second thoughts?

It was a weekend, and I didn't have the girls. I went out that night, and when I got home in the late hours, I called him. *I couldn't believe he was home.* I was in tears and asked him to come over. He drove to my apartment in the middle of the night. I wanted to see if anything remained between us besides our girls. I let him hold me, and we slept. We parted ways the next day, never again to embrace each other with any intimacy and, for me, any regret.

SOFTBALL TIME

A sorority sister asked me to play on a recreational softball team around the same time. *I was a good softball player too!* Absolutely! The team's sponsor was DynaBody, a local gym, and it was made up mostly of firefighters and their friends. We had the first practice at our local state park. My girls were with me, so I drove my car close to the field where I could keep a close eye on them. They sat in the back with the hood open and played while I practiced. A ball went in their direction, nearly hitting my car. The guy retrieving the ball said, "Sorry, that almost hit your car." I looked at him like, where are your priorities?, and said, "I don't care about my car; I just don't want the ball to hit my kids."

SETTLING IN

Small town living wasn't all bad. I began to appreciate the proximity of my job, the girls' daycare, and elementary school to my apartment. I had met new people, made some friends through work, and was still getting to know the ladies in the sorority. I applied for a scholarship with Shawnee Development Council, a social agency that serves the southern seven counties of Illinois. A $500 grant from the agency allowed me to begin college classes in the Fall of 1998. I was starting to fill the pages of my new life.

PART III

Broken–Woman

THESE CHAPTERS ARE RECOLLECTIONS of my experience post-divorce, a post-second petition to move back home, and a new man in my life. They recount specific events that shaped my views of motherhood, dating, and third marriage.

INTERNALLY I WAS BROKEN AND LOST but pretended to be okay. Making the best of a personally sad set of circumstances took effort. Many people showed me kindness and support during this transition. I had closed many doors and turned the page on many of life's chapters. The familiar marriage chapter would present itself again. I said "yes" again at age 34! The early stage of my third marriage could have been better, but it could have been worse. I could have been healthier mentally, but I could have been worse. I was blessed with a "normal" relationship but could not recognize it.

WHAT MATTERS IS THAT WE'RE ALIVE AND WELL.

The New Guy

"It is a truth universally acknowledged, that a single man in possession of a good fortune, must be in want of a wife." —Jane Austen, Pride and Prejudice.

SOFTBALL WIN

*T*HAT GUY ON THE SOFTBALL TEAM WHO WAS CONCERNED about my car was cute.

He was the only single person on the team and a volunteer firefighter. I remember him from that first practice at the park; he was soft-spoken, very athletic, and had a calm demeanor. Initially, my flirty skills didn't work, and it took him a hot minute to ask me out on a date. *I was pretty confident he wanted to go out with me.* One night after practice, a few of us on the team went to a pub for some drinks. We talked a bit at a table, but I became impatient because it was a work night. *I can't stay much longer.* Then my neighbor, Erica, walked in and said, "Hi Sabrina, hi Uncle Robbie."

FIRST DATE

We went to dinner at Applebee's on our first date. I ordered

the steak and a dessert. This date gave us a chance to intro-
duce ourselves. I told him only what I wanted him to know:
where I worked, my home state, a little about why I landed in
Metropolis, my family in Arizona, and how three is a crowd
in a marriage, and I am not about that. In return, he told me
what he wanted me to know. He worked at the water district
for his brother-in-law, lived with his parents, went to a few
different colleges, and graduated with a degree in Nuclear
Engineering in 1993. I didn't know anything about nuclear
engineering, so I asked him to explain. I didn't want another
plutonium-uranium line fed to me. To be our first date, we
had excellent conversations, which led to a second date, plus
we were still playing softball together. We instantly connected on an intellectual level, and he would soon show me the
moon and the stars.

I had many chances to see him around my girls during
summer ball. I liked what I saw: calm, soft-spoken, and a
frank attitude. I didn't feel at all threatened by him. We began
riding to games together. I flat out told him, "Look, I'll date
you through the softball season, and that's it." I was the one
who initiated conversations with my curiosity, but he was
very good with his replies and prompted more questions. I
was especially attracted to his soft-spoken voice. This trait
was a welcoming characteristic. His eyes revealed agree-
ment and dissent, his smile revealed his laughter, and his
presence demonstrated dependability. He felt safe. *I need to
be with someone safe.* I was very interested in what I could
learn from this guy; his knowledge was exciting and attrac-
tive. His good looks and otherwise were simply bonuses. I, on

the other hand, put up a good front. I still sported armor and wondered when he would reveal undesirable characteristics, aka, his bad side.

GOOD LUCK CHARM

Two months after our first date, he began a new job in his chosen career field. This was such good news for him. *I was his good luck charm.* We continued seeing each other through the fall softball season and soon became exclusive. My girls liked him too. One of his firefighter friends, Fudd, told us we had a magnetic attraction to each other. We just clicked.

HIS FAMILY

I didn't want to meet his family right away. That would be too much for me. It would mean moving in a direction that I feared: attachment. I finally met his mom and dad when we celebrated his birthday in July. Later, I met his sister and brother-in-law when my neighbor, Erica, knocked on my door. Something was wrong. With urgency, she told me her brother was in a car accident and asked me to tell her uncle to meet their family at Lourdes Hospital when he got off work.

I met his side of the family when we went there to see if his nephew was okay. Under the circumstances, it was not a time to get to know each other.

His parents and sister kept to themselves going forward unless there was a birthday celebration or a holiday meal to share. They were never intrusive and were very welcoming of my girls and me. They did their thing, and we did ours. We got along well that way.

LIVING ARRANGEMENTS

We were so steady that he asked me to marry him after a few months. *I can handle a long engagement.* The moment was memorable. We went to dinner, went back to my apartment, and I wanted him to leave because I wasn't feeling well. I needed to rest, and he just kept hanging around until finally, he kneeled on the floor next to my bed and pulled out a ring. *At least he had a ring to present.* I had tested this man many times and tried to push him away, but this guy was serious. It may have coincided with plans of moving in together and his desire for an engagement before doing so.

I said yes to both! *You're here so much; you might as well help with the rent.* His parents must have been happy about him moving out because they made sure he didn't forget any of his belongings by helping him pack. We laughed, but there was no going back home for him. He was 31 years old and came with a clean title: no marriages, no children. *Thank goodness.* That meant no exes on his side, making it easier to go forward with an engagement and marriage.

He saw something in me that I did not see. *What does he see in me?* I knew I had some admirable qualities, but I was also wounded inside and had an impressive façade. His problem-solving skills were kicked into high gear when he tried to figure me out. I admit this is a difficult task that is infinitely unsolvable, even for me, and I should have the answer key.

COLLEGE

There were no marriage dates on the calendar because I was determined to finish college first. *I wanted a college degree.* We both had full-time jobs, and I also had the girls to take care of. I attended school full-time with the help of a tuition program at work and Pell Grants from school. I took two classes during my lunch hour and two courses at night. He kept the girls one of the nights, and my ex-mother-in-law (Meme) would keep them on the other night.

I was studying and doing homework when I could find time and wherever I was idle. There was a time when I was in my room reading and my daughter, Victoria, asked me, "Mommy, why are you always doing homework?" I told her I was studying for college now because I did not go right after high school. I tried to relay the message to her that one should go to college before having kids. In hindsight, I think she was sending me a message that she missed me.

I was on course to get my associate degree at the local junior college. Our relationship and living arrangement seemed to be going well. It was nice, and for the most part, we got along well. We were still in the early stages, though, and I was still trying to test his patience and dependability. *He kept passing my tests.* Then we were made aware of an opportunity to buy a house. Rob thought it would be a good idea to be married before we made the purchase. *It was his idea.* He rolled with the flow with me and my control freaki-ness for the most part, but this major step was essential to him. This idea meant something to me too. I was fully aware of the commitment and what that meant to my wanting to get back home. But we felt like a match, and he indeed was a safe place, so I took a leap of faith and decided to get married again.

The Last "I Do"

MARRIAGE

WE WERE MARRIED AT THE COURTHOUSE IN MAY OF 1999, in the same building where I spent so much time trying to get a divorce. *Ironic.* The same judge who granted that divorce performed the contractual ceremony. I wondered if he thought for a moment, "What the heck was she doing back in my courtroom?" If he did, he didn't say, and I didn't ask. I am not making this stuff up! Rob's immediate family was there, including Erica, who would go from neighbor to niece with the words "I Do." This child had an uncle who was single and kind and never tried to set us up. *She didn't think opposites attract.* She saw him as an uncle, and I saw him as a kind, eligible bachelor. We met on our own time and by chance.

When the ceremony was over, we parted ways. Rob and I returned to our respective jobs. One day he was single; the next, he had a wife and two stepdaughters. I left all my former names behind, Gonzales, Jarvis, DeMarco, and became Sabrina Beck.

My girls were part of the deal and attended the ceremony. They were five and three when we met and six and four when we married. We put them to bed that evening, and they shouted, "Good night, Step Daddy!" Lucky girls, now they had two daddies.

ADJUSTING

We moved into our new home as a married couple. We had no honeymoon; instead, we decided the best use for the money was as a down payment. We adjusted to routine married life with our jobs, the girls, and weekends. I continued taking college classes full-time and working full-time. Managing internal stress coupled with expectations, perceived and real, had me relying on less than pleasant coping strategies. I needed silence to concentrate and then became lonely when it was too quiet. I wanted us to be a family and then drew boundaries for parenting my girls. I wanted to feel in love but could not translate Rob's love language. I tried to keep the past locked away, but it seeped out when I began to feel vulnerable. I was a mess. I was going full speed ahead while silently struggling with unresolved pain and a limited number of coping skills.

POSITIVE RESULTS

My junior year in college was almost over when I received the call: "your pregnancy test results are positive." We were going to have a baby, his first, my third. We planned this but did not expect a result so soon. His stoic response to the news had me questioning our decision to have a child. *C'mon, dude, get excited about something.* We did make this decision together; I was there, he was there, we planned.

At three months, the moodiness kicked in, and I began to question if I could do this. I felt overwhelmed with the thought of adding additional responsibilities to my plate because it was changing. Rob continued to get up, get dressed, and leave for work before starting our day. With school, work, kids, and pregnancy, I reached a tipping point and realized I was no superwoman. I was willing to give up school, but he thought it was vital for me to finish my degree. I was ready to quit my job, but that meant I had to rely on unreliable child support and him. The solution: Rob took on the full responsibility of taking care of us girls, and I resigned from the towing company in April 2001. Although, not bringing home a paycheck left me vulnerable and dependent.

On the positive side, the pregnancy was a wonderful, peaceful experience. Aside from some moodiness, it was calm, and I didn't feel alone. I would still wait for Rob to show excitement over our growing baby. He continued his daily morning routine and went to work. At his request, I kept the sex of the baby a secret from him.

IT'S TIME

I was rolling out homemade tortillas on a Sunday evening when my water broke. Since this was my third rodeo, I took my time and showered. Vanessa, who was nine, was concerned that Rob was too calm. He was playing a game on the computer, and she wanted to call 911. Fifty-six minutes after midnight, our daughter was born. He was there the whole time.

He didn't say much, but he was there. I guess he was scared and didn't know what to do. After the birth, he sat quietly in my hospital room and would ask if he could do anything for me. *We just had a baby. Can you do a backflip, please?* The stench of his chewing tobacco set me off, and I wanted him out of my room! I spent that night alone in the hospital.

My frame of mind when taking our baby home was highly sensitive. *I just expected him to be a little more vocally excited about the birth of our baby.* He was off work for the next two weeks for baby leave. I had hoped having an extra set of hands would be helpful. My expectations were high, and his initiative was low. I considered his age instead of inexperience, and I was hard on him. Why wasn't he able to voice that he needed help and not criticism. *He may have, and I was just pissed by then.* My "I can do this by myself" mindset trapped me, and he was only in my way. I felt this way for no reason other than his silence and passiveness. *Jump in the damn boat with me, dude!*

My marriage to Rob was stable, and it did not come with abusive behavior or infidelity. We didn't even really drink or have alcohol in the home. It was peaceful, calm, and routine. This home environment was not normal to me. I still couldn't understand how I felt lonely when I was with a man who was present, respectful, kind, loving, and caring. I created chaos when it could have been a shared learning experience between an experienced mother and a new father.

I was not adept at the nuclear family. He was. For me to tell a grown-ass adult man what to do was extra for me. We lived in the same house, slept in the same room, ate in the same kitchen, sat in the same living room. *Look around and see what is out of place and fix it!* I was overwhelmed and exhausted. I couldn't even finish the school semester, so I dropped that class. I was hard on myself and even harder on him. But he was still there.

A LITTLE ROOM

I moved out of our bedroom and into one of the girls' bedrooms, moving them into sharing a room in a move that resembled a flight. I did not have enough energy to give him a lesson in life while managing the other people in the household. It was he and I, and we were on our own. I would continue to plea for him to communicate with me on an emotional level. *Use your words! I want to hear you!* I was hungry for a two-way adult relationship with the man I married and was supposed to spend the rest of my life with. I expressed how his silence induced loneliness in me that wasn't easy to handle. It didn't seem fair that I put myself in this marital bond of trust, yet he did not trust me enough to be more open with me. *I was so emotional.* The in-house separation lasted about two weeks, and then we reunited in the same bed and pushed on with life together.

HIS STORY

Indeed, there were explanations for his quietness, but he didn't share them. I know I was rough and frustrated, but I also invited him to let me in many times. I let him know I needed a connection. I was left to fill in the blanks. I only knew of a broken engagement and a life-changing accident that had long-lasting consequences. I conjectured that he had yet to forgive himself, which was the cause of his inward disposition with life. I guess I was not the only one who had a history.

MY MAN

He was the only man I wanted to interact with and the only one I was around. I was home with the kids all day just like I wanted. I didn't know it would come at the cost of adult interaction. When he came home from work, I wanted interaction in the evenings, and I got a lot of silence.

My pleadings would continue, and I would repeat, "I give up," and "I'm not going to go through this again." I tried being silent, "Fine, I'll just exist in the same house as you and take care of my kids and me." I tried, many times, using my loudest voice because then maybe he could hear me. I wanted to keep busy with part-time jobs here and there where I met some fabulous people, only to resign for various reasons.

COFFEE MORNINGS

I had two girlfriends whom I bonded with for a few years. Our families would get together on special occasions for meals and fun; *us* wives would have coffee connections and chat about the local scuttlebutt and complain about our husbands. We would go out for lunch and go shopping too. Then life became busy with jobs and other interests, and we wouldn't meet as much and then not at all. This interaction was ideal for a while and had filled a void in my life.

COLLEGE

After five years of pursuing higher education, I graduated from college with a Bachelor of Science in Workforce, Education, and Development. It was such a proud moment for me personally, and it was nice to have my husband and daughters present to witness this accomplishment. *I wish my mom could see this.* We all made sacrifices to get to this moment. The expense of time, money, energy, emotions, and detours wore on us.

No more school; I was free to focus only on being a wife and mother. But I could not be still. I used my degree to work as a substitute teacher to keep busy. It was convenient, and the schedule allowed me to drop off and pick up my girls from school. I went searching outside my home for an essential human connection. What I wanted was a deeper connection with my husband.

A BIGGER PLACE

In August of 2002, we moved from our first home in the city to a bigger house in a county neighborhood. Everyone would have their room, plus we had a guest room. The distance was only 3.2 miles away from the small town I felt trapped in, with a population of 14,995 in 2001, and it has been decreasing ever since. I drove my girls into town to the same city school so they would not have to change peer groups. Graciela, my youngest daughter, was pre-kindergarten age and refused to attend. She preferred "mommy's school" at home.

VACATIONS

I needed to stay connected to my family and fill my peace cup. While it wasn't entirely unfair to my husband and girls, it wasn't bad. He also enjoyed Arizona. We did go to the Grand Canyon, Tucson's Wild West Show, city shopping, dining, and swimming in a hotel pool in November.

We would take mini-vacations to the St. Louis Zoo and Science Center when in Illinois. We continue to have a membership with the Arizona Science Center.

KEEP BUSY

If I kept busy enough, I could ignore my inner struggles with loneliness. I tried 'at home' self-employment jobs, coached my daughter's basketball team, taught gymnastics, performed in community theater, and did other volunteer activities in the community. One year I was an 'Angry Vagina' when I volunteered for *The Vagina Monologues* play. My mom, sister, brother, and best friend came out to see me. I was busy with activities. All things that would seem normal, and they were, but I still felt alone. I would go in, fill the activity, and return to my humble abode. I couldn't make any further connections with folks, wasn't connecting with my husband at home, and my family was still so far away in Arizona. No matter how busy I kept myself, I could not fill the void of the family. Something still seemed to be missing.

CONSISTENCY

Rob remained consistent in his role as a provider and step-dad. He worked, offered to take us out to dinner, stayed up and tutored the girls with homework, would pick them up from dances, and was at all their extra-curricular activities. He did and continues to do so much more for our girls.

He walked in the door from work at 4:00 p.m. every day. If he got a fire call, he would call to tell me where he was. At times, I would become irritated at this. His consistency confused me. I suggested he go to the gym or hang out with his friends after work. "You don't always have to come straight home." Insane suggestions all because of my discomfort with "normal."

I wanted him to take over cooking dinner to relieve me from my never-ending housewife duties. *I know, poor me.* He would take us out to dinner instead. This alternative should have been a welcomed solution, but I felt he was skirting the moment to see what it was like in my shoes. *Show me, don't buy me.*

Parenting teenage girls soon became problematic, especially juggling their relationship with Vince, their dad. My constant need to be the only one to parent my girls was not helpful. I was drowning in the challenges that came with divorced parenting. Rob was always on standby mode, ever-present to help, but I stubbornly would not reach for the life ring. They were my responsibility.

We slept in the same bed together, but emotionally I remained miles away. By now, I was having issues with intimacy. I thought if I could get more of his words, I would feel more comfortable while we were in bed. Ironically, I was in bed a lot. I was tired and didn't realize that was a symptom of depression. I blamed it on the disconnect. I blamed many things on him. *Why can't he fix my feelings!*

All he wanted to do was take care of me, and I wouldn't let him. Not completely. I did not want anything except his words and emotions, and they were too few. I was becoming more and more empty inside and wanted more and more to be back home in Arizona. I did strive to make a life here with him the best I could and with the life tools I had in my sketchy toolbox. My DB was too heavy, and I was consistently sabotaging our relationship with angry cries of loneliness. I was losing myself to his continued consistency of kindness, dependability, and presence to normal.

OVER THE YEARS

My pleadings would return, and we would both take steps forward and then steps backward. My husband could not read my mind, nor would I let him in; the DB was mine, and no one would take it away from me. Time and time again, I felt in a situation difficult to deal with and get out of, and I couldn't shake the feeling of being stuck.

He made attempts at spending quality time together. We made two trips to a resort for a weekend getaway. We didn't talk up a storm to each other, but we both had a chance to relax and enjoy the weekend. We had no other responsibilities except to enjoy the getaway and the planned activities, cooking class, yoga, and couple's massage. He purchased season tickets to the Tennessee Performing Arts Center (TPAC) plays and even arranged a couple of overnight stays at a hotel. The girls even got in on the theater action by taking turns attending plays. As much as it was time for Rob and me, it was also nice to get away with one of the girls and give them undivided attention. *I've seen Wicked three times.*

This man was trying to give me things that I loved, and it was working. This effort gave us content to talk about. We were talking about everything else except us. He remained emotionally closed off. *I blamed him.* I still had too much silence in my head and loneliness in my heart. I even told him I would ride this out until our youngest daughter was 18; I would then leave and escape to Arizona.

LIFE WAS A MESS

He began going to counseling in Paducah, Kentucky, with Mr. George Kyle, a mental health counselor located in an office at a housing unit. Rob went to him a few times, and I went once. I didn't particularly care for him. We were having behavioral issues with our middle daughter, and we thought it would be good to have her go to counseling. Rob took her to an appointment with George Kyle. It didn't go well, and she refused to go back. She became even more resentful. I didn't know they arrested this sick man later for running an alternative "sex therapy" business at a local hotel. *That bastard!* All I knew was that she refused to go to counseling.

Working Overtime

WORKING AGAIN

WHEN LIFE GETS ROUGH, I GET A JOB, TWO, OR THREE. At one time, I worked as a gymnastics instructor, substitute teacher, and helper at a local daycare. I added to this load by accepting a part-time job as a reporter for a radio station. I found out about a full-time job opening as a manager for a bus transportation company through this job. I applied, interviewed, and got hired. I began working at the end of May 2008. I worked beyond overtime all summer long to ensure the students would have transportation to and from school. Bus transportation was a big deal in our small town, and it wouldn't be an easy transition. Bus drivers were upset that the contract went to an out-of-town student transportation company, and I wanted to see if I could help with that transition. This job would turn out to be a bigger mess for our family.

I became obsessed with doing a good job. I would focus on something new and ignore the problems at home. The summer passed by quickly. It brought me joy to have something of my own, but the rest of the family was unhappy with my new attitude. We had a family meeting, and that didn't go well. I told them I was moving out. I could finally afford to support myself, and I would fix our problems by moving the girls and me into our own place, except that neither of the older girls wanted to move. They would rather stay in the big house with their stepdad than move to a new smaller place with their mom.

THE GIRLS

During this time, our girls saw their mother planning an escape. *I couldn't see their view of the situation.* They didn't have to directly experience the divorce between their dad and me when they were younger. They were 16 and 14 and fully aware of the fallout from separation and potentially divorce.

Their dad mainly was in and sometimes out of the picture. *I don't know where he is, but I know he loves you, girls.* I tried to normalize their father-daughter relationships. We would accommodate him whenever he wanted to see them, but we didn't know when. If he became absent, their grandmother Meme would pick them up. She loved her grandbabies and was always there for them, while there was always something going on with Vince.

THEIR DAD

I had moved out of our home and into another house in town. It was smaller and much easier to take care of. Vince had stopped by the new house when the girls were in school. I am sure the girls had filled him in on the latest happenings with their mom. Even though we were two unqualified people to talk about marriage issues, we talked about my current marital situation. I gave him the brief form from my point of view, and he threw me off with a surprising response. He told me to give Rob a chance because he was a good guy and was good to our girls. He added that I should think about it before making any big decisions. Out of all the wrongs of our marriage, he turned out to be right this time.

LAY OFF

Rob and I talked about downsizing our home in the mix of things. Although, I was the only one who felt this way. When I moved out, I could not purchase a home on my own, and Rob insisted that it be in both our names, but the salary from my job would pay for it. Things took a drastic turn three weeks after living on my own when my employer let me go.

The company laid me off under the guise of budget cuts. And that may have been true, but I would find out later that other employees may have played an active role in seeing that I was gone. Small town drama is for the natives, and it sucks. It was very odd how this happened; my supervisor came down from the main office, cleared the office area out, presented me with an empty box, and said, "We are laying you off as of today." I was so dumbfounded that I said, "Oh, okay, do you want me to finish off the day?" "No, you need to leave now."

THE FALL OUT

The fallout reared like a set of dominos; I lost the means to support myself and had to relinquish the company car. My eldest daughter had been using my car, and now she would have to return it. I could have waited until she got home from school to get the car, but I went to get it in the middle of the school day. She was angry about this and the many other decisions I had made recently. I was not thinking right, I was spiraling down, and then I fell.

It was Rob who came to my rescue. I was upset, but the girls were furious and did not want to see me or talk to me. I believed they no longer wanted anything to do with me; I thought I had lost them. I was unable to process what was happening to my world. One day I thought I had the answer to my problems, and the next, I was the problem.

TO BE OR NOT TO BE

I was so distraught that I concluded I had lost my girls. After all these years, the heartache, the battling to keep them safe, the sacrifice of staying in Illinois, it was too much. All this, and I could not keep them safe from me.

For a moment, the earth was flat, and I had barely the desire to hang on to the edge. I quickly came up with a plan and shared this with Rob through sobbing and tears. I would leave our daughter with him, and the older girls could go live with their dad. Then, I would go home and live a life far enough away not to hurt them anymore. I would let go and give it all up. I could no longer hold it together. I needed help. *National Helpline 1-800-662- HELP (4357).*

THE ELEPHANT

I am not sure if I called my primary care physician for a referral or if I called myself. With insurance, I am sure I needed a referral. I landed at CenterPointe Behavioral Health System, a treatment facility. I walked in there with the weight of an elephant. Through the CBT process, I left with new tools in my toolbox and less junk in my DB.

The older girls stayed with their Meme and dad during the early process. Rob took care of Graciela and me.

PART IV

Soul–Broken

THESE CHAPTERS ARE RECOLLECTIONS of my experience with cognitive behavioral therapy. They recount specific steps that shaped my views of mental health, interpersonal relationships, and purging past pains.

I WANTED OUT OF THE DARKNESS. I was ready to face the broken parts of me. I made the best of my time in therapy and did the work to get back to me. The many professionals guiding my care and treatment to release the skewed views of events I carried in my DB and of myself were a blessing. I didn't have to let go of the traumas, but I did. My therapeutic journey could have been better, but it could have been worse. I could have been a better patient, but I could have been worse. Having medical insurance —although still costly— and dedicating time to the six-week treatment was imperative. I remain eternally grateful to my supportive husband, pastor, and family; I would have stayed down for the count without all of them.

WHAT MATTERS IS THAT I AM ALIVE AND WELL.

Identity Crisis

*I want my kids back. I want my kids
back. I want my kids back. —Me.*

EMPTINESS

ITHOUT MY KIDS, I FELT I HAD NO OTHER VALUABLE
identity. When I became a mother, my life gained
purpose, and I felt reborn as a human being. I would never
feel alone again.

As a daughter, I felt abandoned; as a mother, I over-parented; as a younger sibling, I felt forgotten; as a wife, I felt
unpartnered; as a best friend, I was too far away; as a co-worker, I was temporary.

Who was I now? What hole did I fall through, and whom
would I be when and if I came out of it? I had no plan; my life
tank was empty, and I wanted to give up entirely. *I can't leave
my girls.* I could not do more to them than I already had. After
years of pushing through life with my DB in tow, it was time
to dump it. It was getting in the way of my relationship with
my husband and children. I didn't have any more masks to
wear. This moment is where the journey out of depression

began. It would require me to dig deep, dust off, and do the work to win them back and discover my self-worth. I needed this to get my girls back.

OUTPATIENT PATIENT

On October 29, 2008, I was admitted to a program on an outpatient schedule at CenterPointe that required my participation from 9:00 a.m. to 2:00 p.m., five days a week. It was a behavioral health extension of Lourdes Hospital in Paducah, Kentucky, and included CBT. I had time to take the kids to school (although the older girls got rides most of the time), drive to Paducah, check-in as an outpatient, attend treatment, eat lunch, go back to treatment, and return with enough time to pick the kids up from school. The process included an Outpatient Daily Check-In, a brief meeting with the psychiatrist, group therapy, individual therapy session, and vitals check by the nurse.

DAILY CHECK-IN

Each day upon arrival, I would fill out a one-page daily check-in sheet. I self-reported a number between one and ten about how I felt that day. Levels of depression, anger, anxiety, shame, pain, binge/substance abuse, appetite, energy level, suicidal/self-harm, hallucinations, sleep, medication compliance, side effects, and critical or stressful issues of the day. There was room to comment on how self-responsible I was with my treatment and a brief comment on a daily positive affirmation for myself over the last 24 hours. A bit much for someone who was majorly depressed and anxious about life.

It gave me pause to think about all those aspects I had ignored until this time in my life. Perhaps it was a necessary tool for staff to organize prompts in therapy sessions. Remember, this was self-reporting and could only be as effective as one is willing to submit honest self-assessments daily. I was all in for the treatment process as I had everything to lose and everything to gain.

MEDICATION MEETING

I met with the psychiatrist. He made an initial assessment of my symptoms, learned of my medical history, and assigned a diagnosis and treatment plan. Subsequent meetings did not last that long. He asked how I was feeling, if I was experiencing any side effects from the medication he prescribed, and decided whether to continue prescribing medication. *I don't like pills.* He prescribed Lexapro, a Selective Serotonin Reuptake Inhibitor (SSRI), to treat depression and generalized anxiety disorder (GAD). I was depressed, anxious, and worn the hell out. The medication helped calm the restless and irrational thoughts my depression and anxiety were causing.

GROUP THERAPY

I attended group therapy in the morning and the afternoon with others who were there for reasons of their account. We were not to share personal information or stories told during the group discussions. If we were to encounter anyone outside of a group in public, we were to maintain privacy. This method worked for me because, frankly, the way I felt, I did not want to talk to anyone.

We would take turns and share a little about why we were there. This sharing time is where you can become aware that you are not alone in your struggles. Because my world came crashing down, I didn't think anyone else could understand my dilemma. I was wrong. We sincerely helped each other. I could see the struggles of others with a clear lens but was unable to use those lenses on mine. They could see mine, and sharing reverberated the healing process. It was a safe, goal-oriented, supportive environment. I had a hard time accepting that my experiences with Rob were because of my past traumas. I soon accepted that Rob was a safe place, that I had survived my past, and had love and support.

In one group therapy session, I addressed the big fat elephant in my world: my mistrust of men. There had been a trail of men who had hurt me, leaving only the memories of disgust, shame, and worthlessness. I learned that I was projecting this onto my husband, Rob. He was never any of those things. He was taciturn but a gentleman, the most supportive husband and stepfather, and a provider. He was the real deal, and I treated him as if he were them. I could not detach from my past bag of pain to accept the things and people right in front of me.

In another session, I had a hard time facing a personal truth. It was about my mom. The hardest thing to do is to talk about your momma! Careful now. Somehow the counselor picked up on some hidden feelings about my relationship with my mother. I childishly turned from her, pouted a bit, and shut down. I shut down. We later talked about it in an individual session. I discovered that part of my loneliness had to do with the feeling of abandonment by my mom. I say that but simultaneously begin the excuses: she was a working, single mother supporting her children who experienced depression, distrusted men, and did the best she could; I was the one who moved away. It was my fault that I chose to leave the country, marry into the military, follow my husband (Vince) across the country, and ended up over 1600 miles away from my family, raising my daughters by myself. I did this to myself. All that may be true. It didn't change how I felt—an enormous feeling of abandonment and loneliness.

INDIVIDUAL THERAPY

This therapy was a time to focus on myself as a person. I could share more specifics that I could not or would not share in group therapy. We all have that something that we will never tell anyone, except maybe your therapist, who is obligated to your privacy. This therapy is where we cry the most and make some self-realizations. I learned a few life skills; that medication alone is not the answer; there is no set time frame of treatment that indicates you have achieved your healing, and it is an ongoing process determined only by your progress.

DISCHARGED

On November 21, 2008, I was discharged with a continuing care plan and experiencing ongoing depressed mood and anxiety. There were recommendations for medication and counseling for the continuation of treatment. I was referred to Merit Behavioral Health to see a psychiatrist (Dr. Burba, in Mayfield, KY), and a licensed clinical social worker (T.

Shanahan) five days after discharge. I would drive 45 minutes from home to receive counseling and was grateful for reliable transportation and the resources to pay for gas and fees.

IT WAS WORTH IT

It was tough but worth it! Through CBT, I learned to navigate the inner pathways of my thoughts, feelings, and emotions that were killing me deep inside. I discovered what it was to be emotionally stunted and realized that my level of development did not match my age. I had things happen to me in my formative years that I could not explain. I was so busy living in survival mode that I did not recognize the unhealthy strategies I had adopted. I wasn't a bad person or a particularly sad person. There were occasions, circumstances, and situations in life that threw me curves, and I did not have the tools to manage or process them properly. These events created experiences and had a profound effect on my psyche.

SUPPORT FROM THE OUTSIDE

My Husband. He remained consistently supportive, understanding, and insightful. He suffered during this time as well but remained ever-present.

My Pastor. When I moved out, he took the time to visit me. After some discussion, he asked but one thing of me: not to make any decisions (about divorce) right now. I agreed because I had the utmost respect for him as a person and pastor; I credit his "counsel" for saving me from another divorce.

My Friends. Few as there were, they allowed me the time and space needed to work through this season of life. Others seemed shocked by my uncertainty. Why would I want to divorce Rob? If they judged me, they did not express it to me.

My Sister Gigi. I would not have many conversations with her. I didn't feel she understood what was going on with me. While I was not privy to her conversations with my husband during this time, she would later tell me she told Rob he should divorce my ass. The flight runs in our family.

My In-Laws. They did not say a word, speak to me about it or talk to me at all. My father-in-law made a few appearances but kept his thoughts to himself. If there was any judgment on me, it was not to my face. Later, through small talk only, I discovered that my sister-in-law was confused about why I would want to leave her brother. She was unaware of my past, so that was understandable.

My Ex. The girls stayed with their dad and their Meme while I went through this process. I had talked to Vince before this breakdown happened, and he thought I should stay with Rob. There were still pending issues to deal with our middle daughter, but I was glad he was there to help them. I think he wanted to help them. His mom sure was. I knew the girls would be in good hands through this challenging time.

Some around me had given me counsel and allowed me the space to breathe, and others may have taken advantage of this vulnerable moment in my life. Years later, my husband would tell me that people he knew advised him to divorce me. I am glad he didn't listen to them.

GETTING BACK UP

When one gets down from a knockout, trips, or falls, as happened to me, we need to make choices. I could have stayed knocked down and given up. I wonder if that was the point where I could have gone AWOL, as many people do. I could have forged forward on the same dung bag road. But I didn't have the energy to be angry for life, and I wanted more. I chose to seek help. I could do it on my own. If I kept busy enough, I could ignore all the hurt. At 43, the stuff in my DB had caught up to me. It stunk! My choice was goal-oriented: I wanted my girls back, and with hard work and support, I got more than that; I got *me* back.

Blue Folder Drawings

DRAWING WAS NEVER MY FORTE. I AM NOT AN ARTIST. Heck, I change my handwriting pattern based on my moods. Graphologists would have a field day with my writing and my drawings. It is difficult for me to keep still. So, I brought a drawing pad and pencil with me to doodle while at the same time participating in the program. This activity helped me process emotions when I could not verbalize them. I would pour my feelings out onto paper. They came from a deep, neurobiological place where memories are managed, or in my case, mismanaged.

I have put most of these experiences in their proper place and context through therapy and time. RIP adverse life events! My drawings, kept in a blue folder for 13 years, reflect some of those experiences.

As I studied each sketch, I attempted to briefly explain the thoughts or feelings I experienced at that moment. Since we can perceive art subjectively, the backstories of each drawing are in the next chapter, *Backstories for the Drawings*.

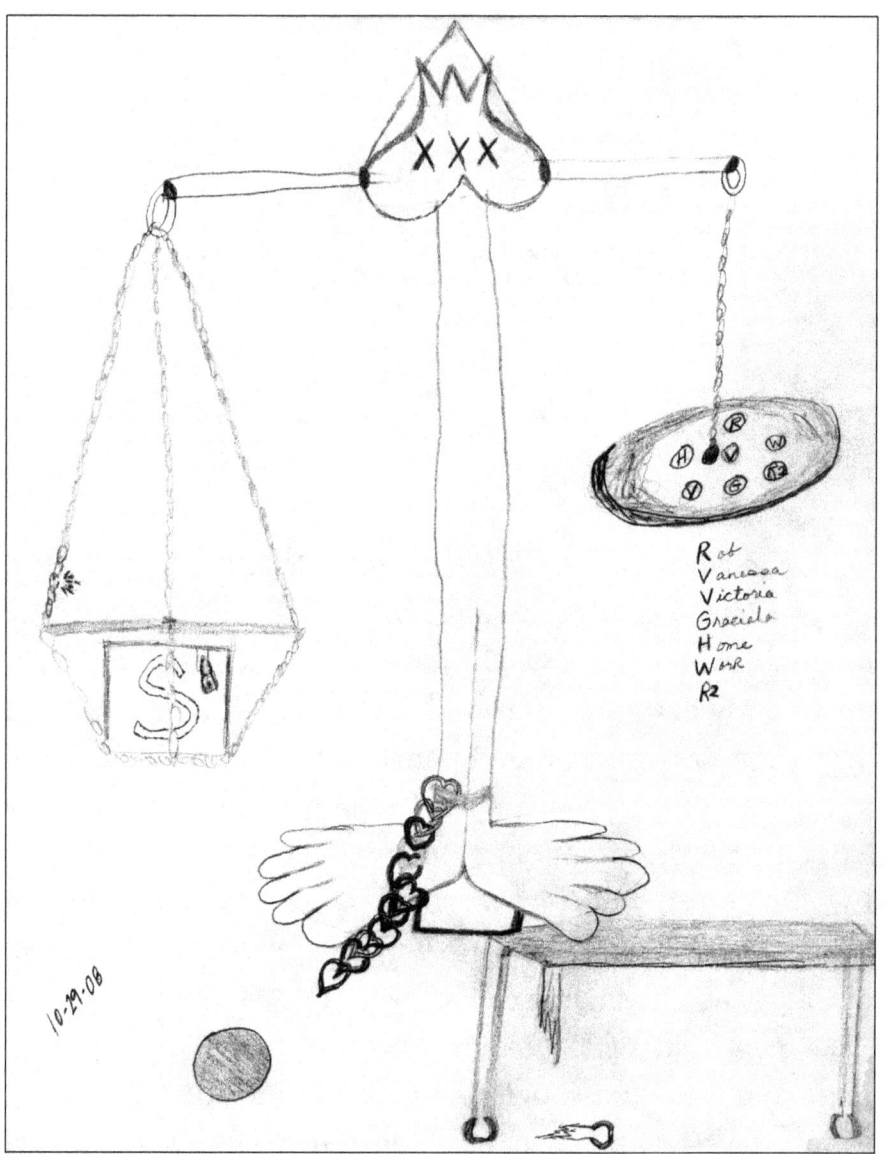

BALANCE OF DECEPTION

*The balancing act I forged over the years was
faltering. It was always a balance of deception.*

DARE TO LOVE

My marriage was burning down. He dared to love me through the fire.

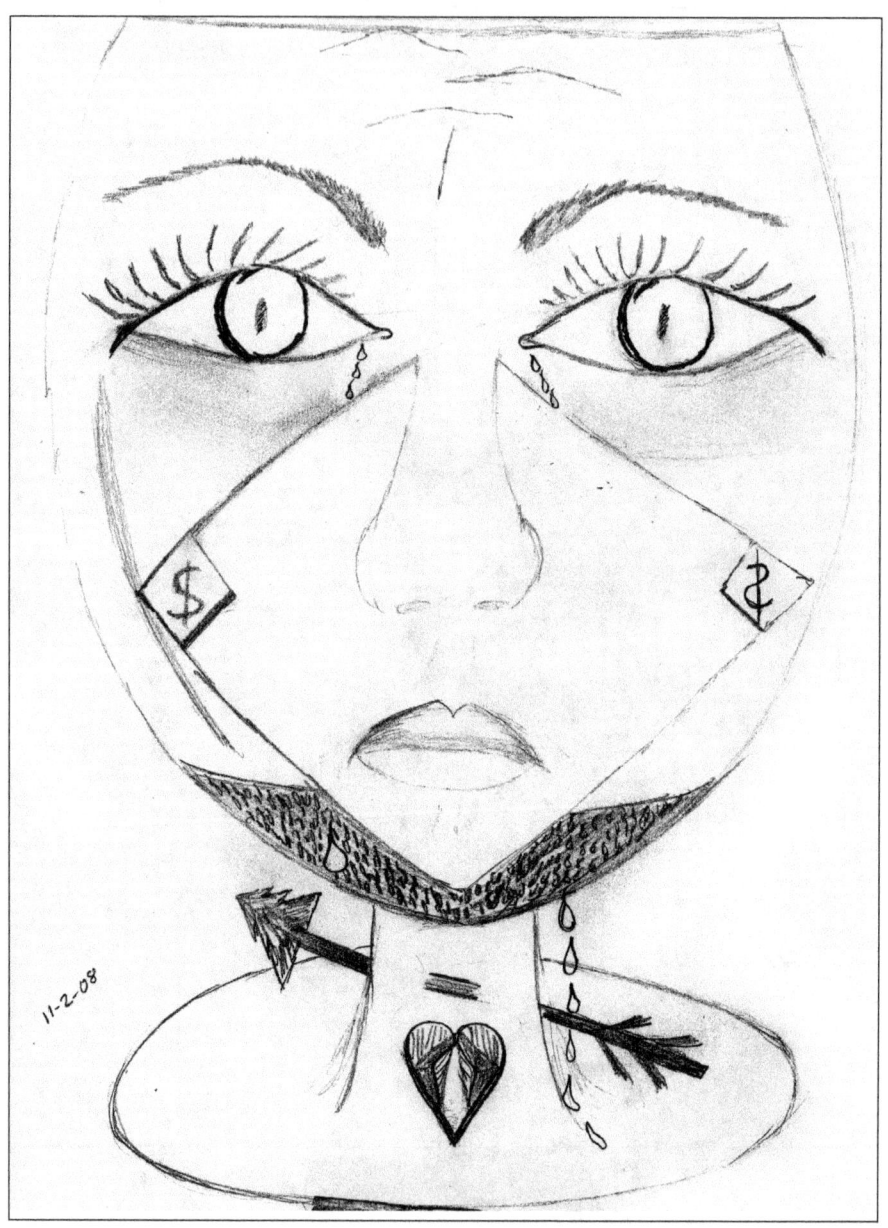

TRAPPED IN TEARS

I felt trapped in my tears and fears. It was suffocating.

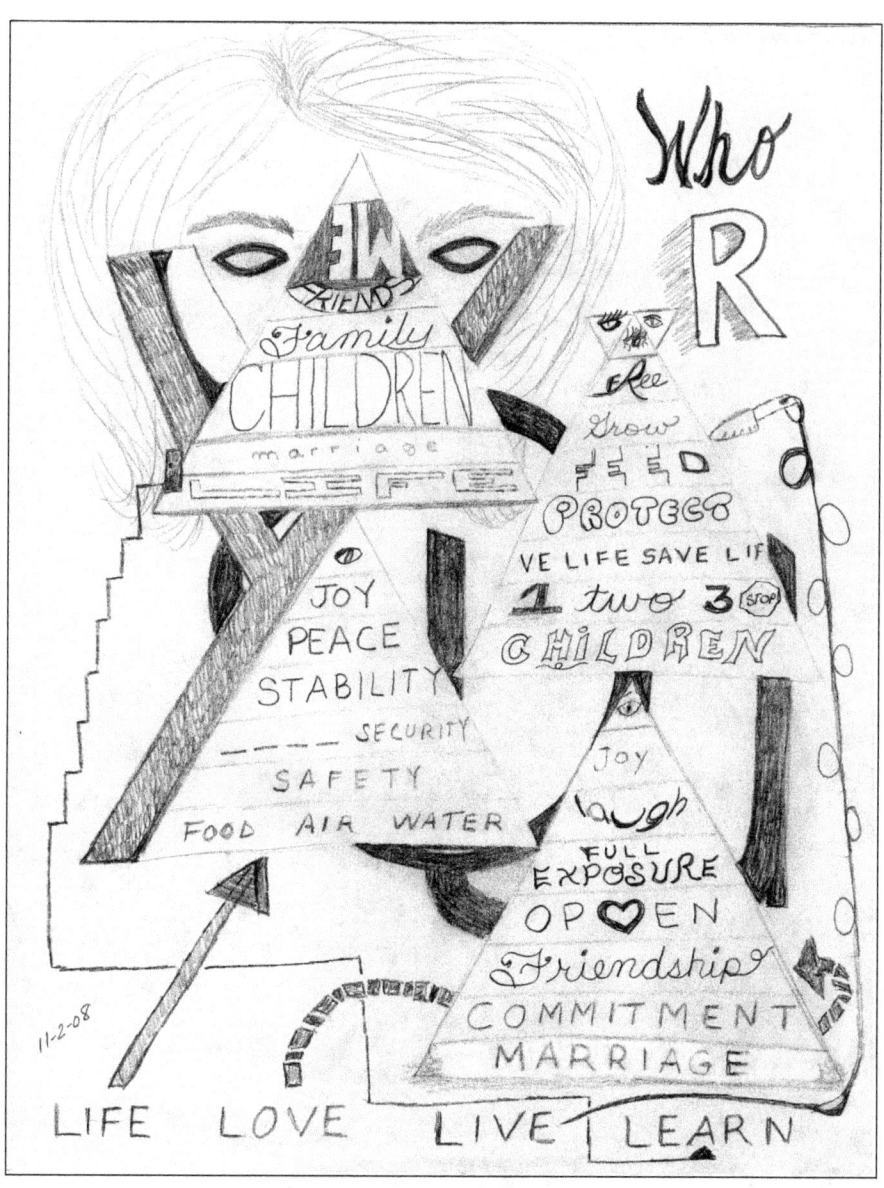

THE SELF

On the run for so long, I never paused to consider who I was or wanted to be. Complexity was unavoidable.

DEAR FAMILY

Dear Family, please grant me patience. I am
working hard to get back to you.

A Peace of Time

*How much time was I giving outwardly? It
brought me joy, but did it bring me peace?*

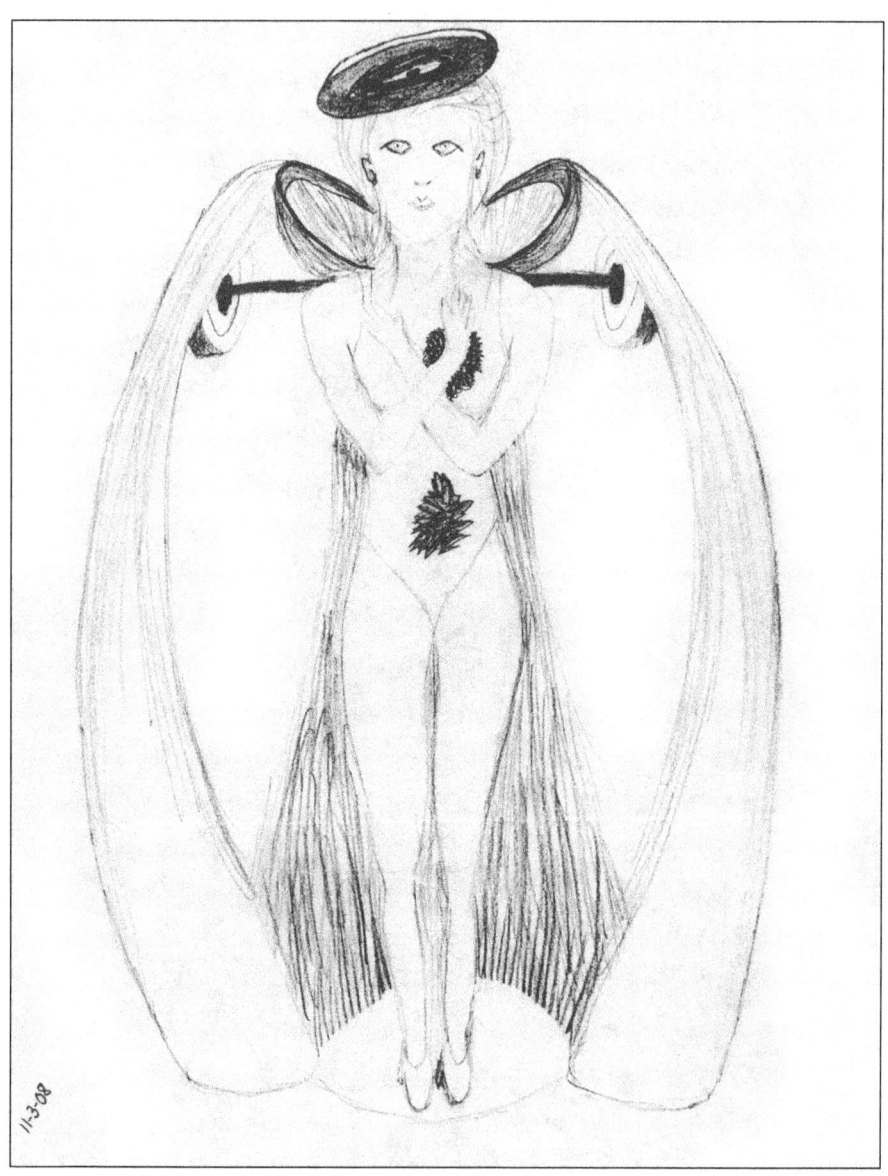

COVERED IN PAIN

A woman who hides her pain carries the load alone.

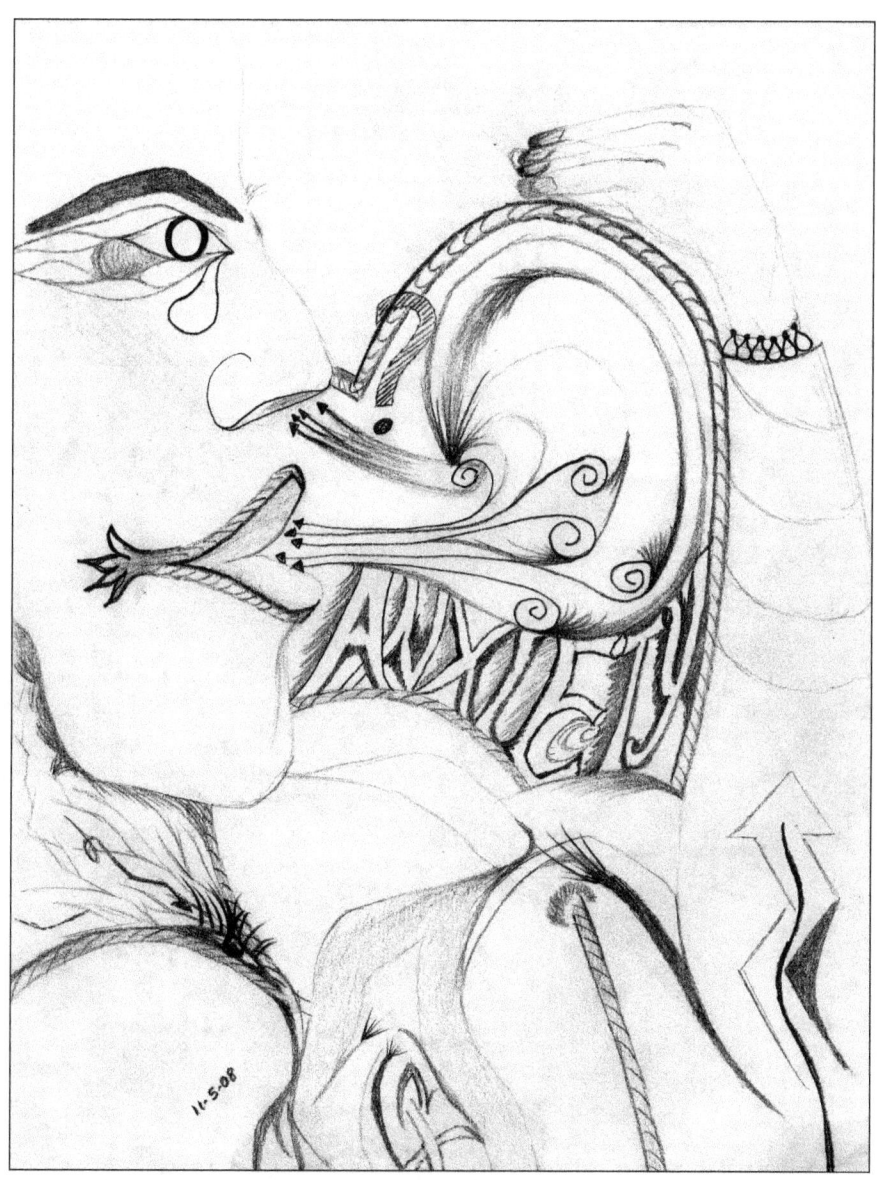

ANXIETY

*We cannot explain anxiety easily. It creeps up on you, sucks
your breath away, and hangs around for an unspecified time.*

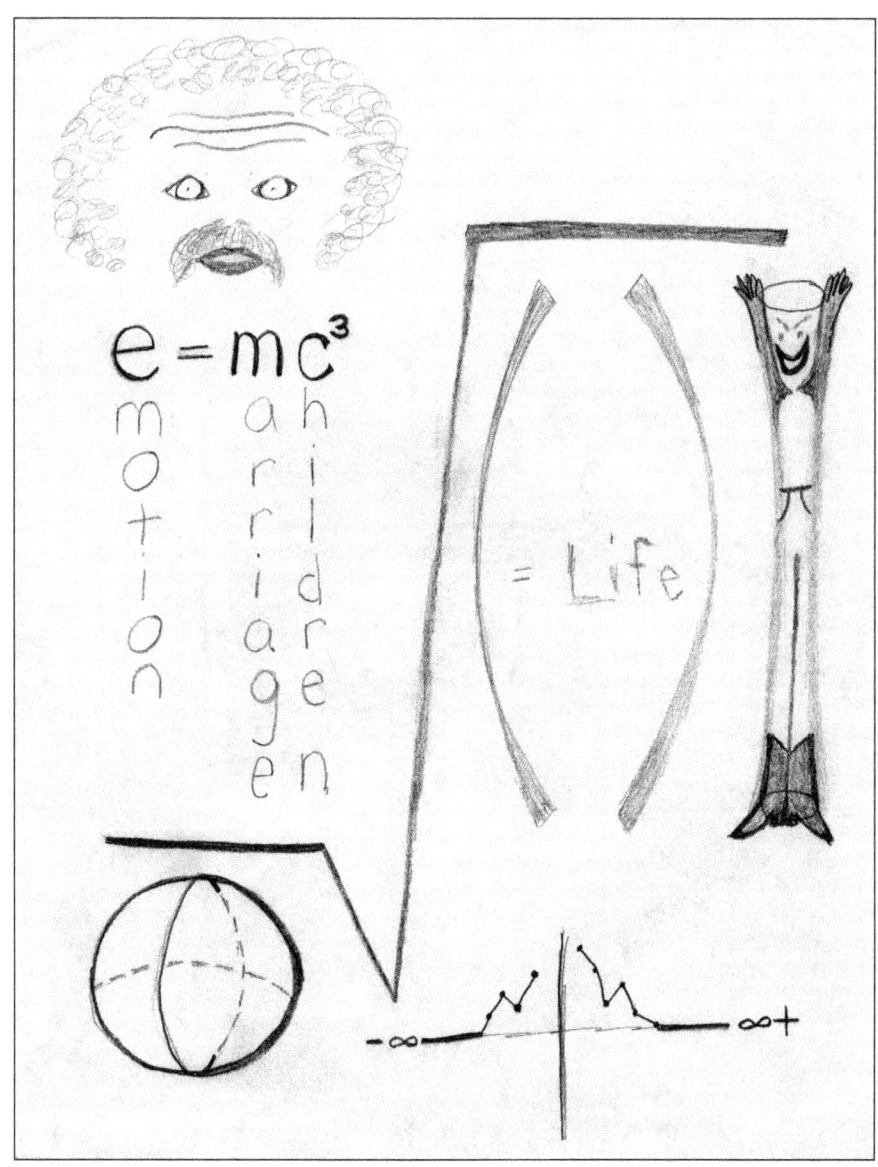

I'M NO EINSTEIN

*A left-brain man and a right-brain woman walk
into a marriage. Let the translation begin.*

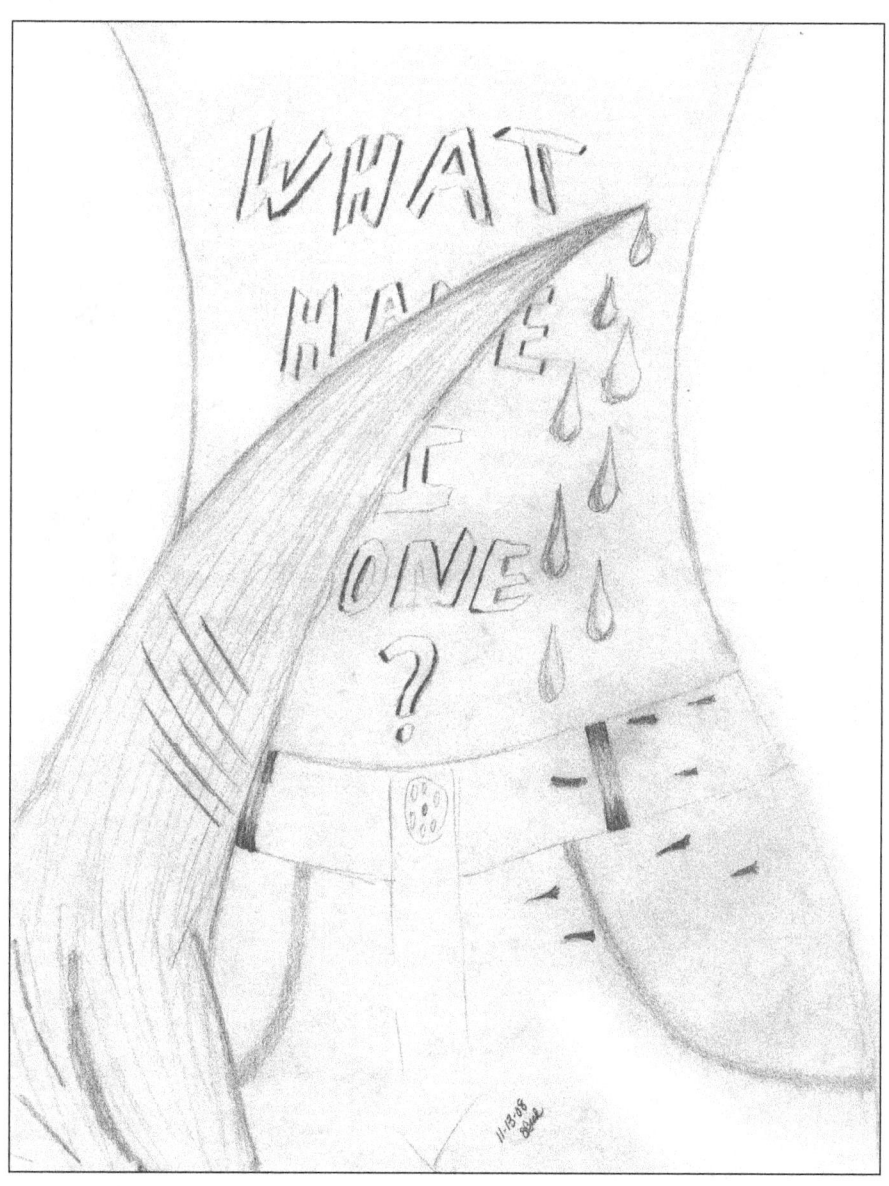

WHAT HAVE I DONE?

I was not the only one hurting. She was cutting herself, and I didn't know.

HAMLET

Time stood still when I lost my girls—all released slings and arrows.
There was work to be done to overcome the hurt in them and me.

IT'S NOT ABOUT ME

Spend time focusing on others and avoid dealing with your issues.

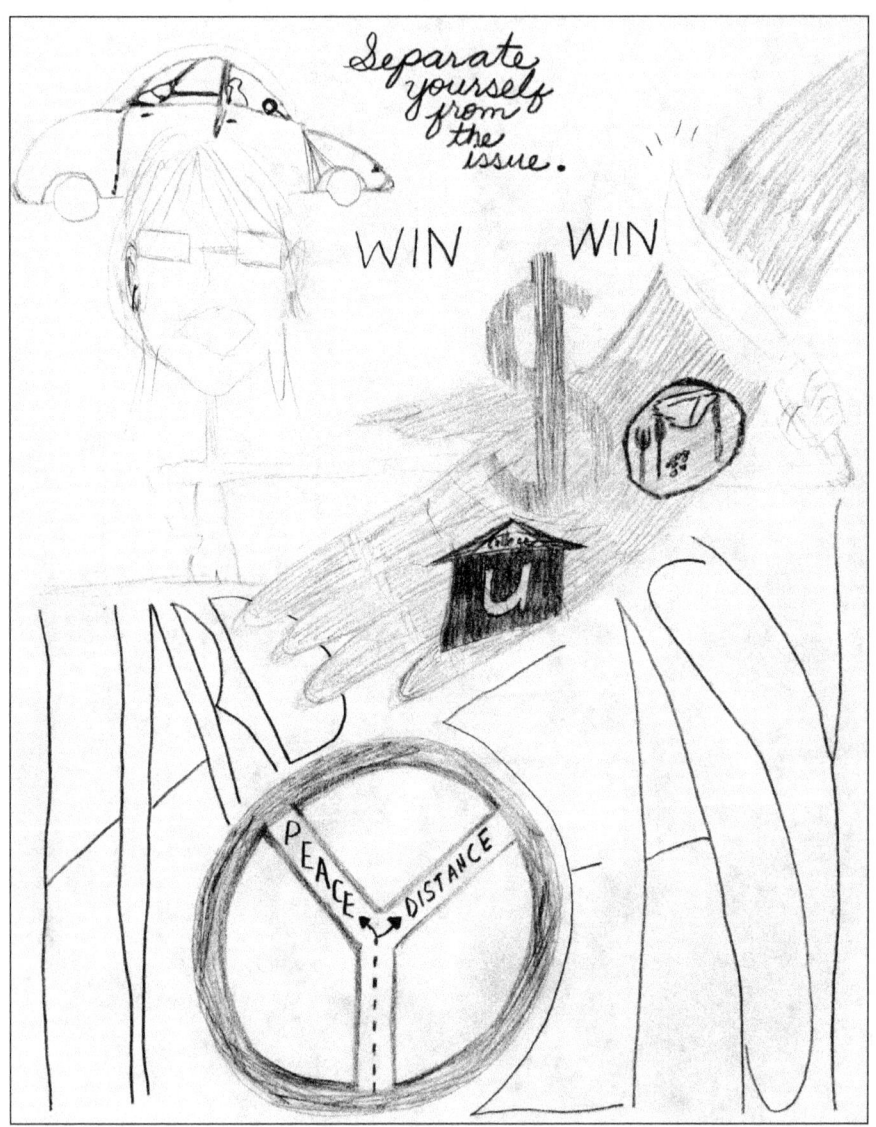

TOOLBOX 101

I buried the most disturbing things of my life deep into my psyche. My life strategy toolbox was minuscule. When given guidance and feedback in therapy, I found it easier to separate myself from the issue.

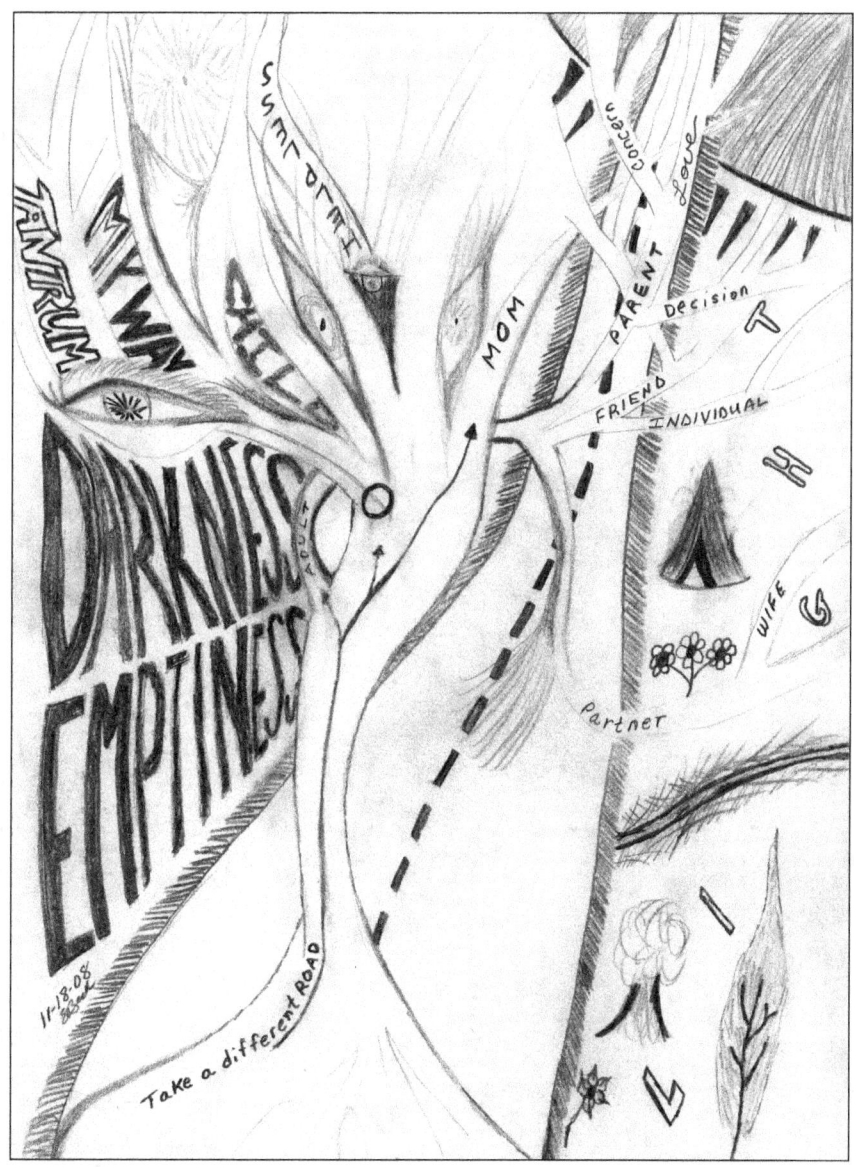

TOOLBOX 102

When the road you have traveled becomes worn and consistently leads to dead ends, consider another direction to reach a bountiful destination.

SOMETIMES

It was easier for me to do it myself until it wasn't. It was challenging but relieving when I could admit that I needed help sometimes.

NOT ALONE

Leaning in with group therapy. I didn't have to hide any longer.

INJURIES

My injuries, perceived or real, felt like arrows through my heart. As the arrows landed, some remained in a dark place. I needed help to get out of the darkness.

I'M FINE!

A smile conveys a positive emotion, right? It also takes fewer muscles to smile than to make a frown. So why not smile and keep everyone out. HELP ME.

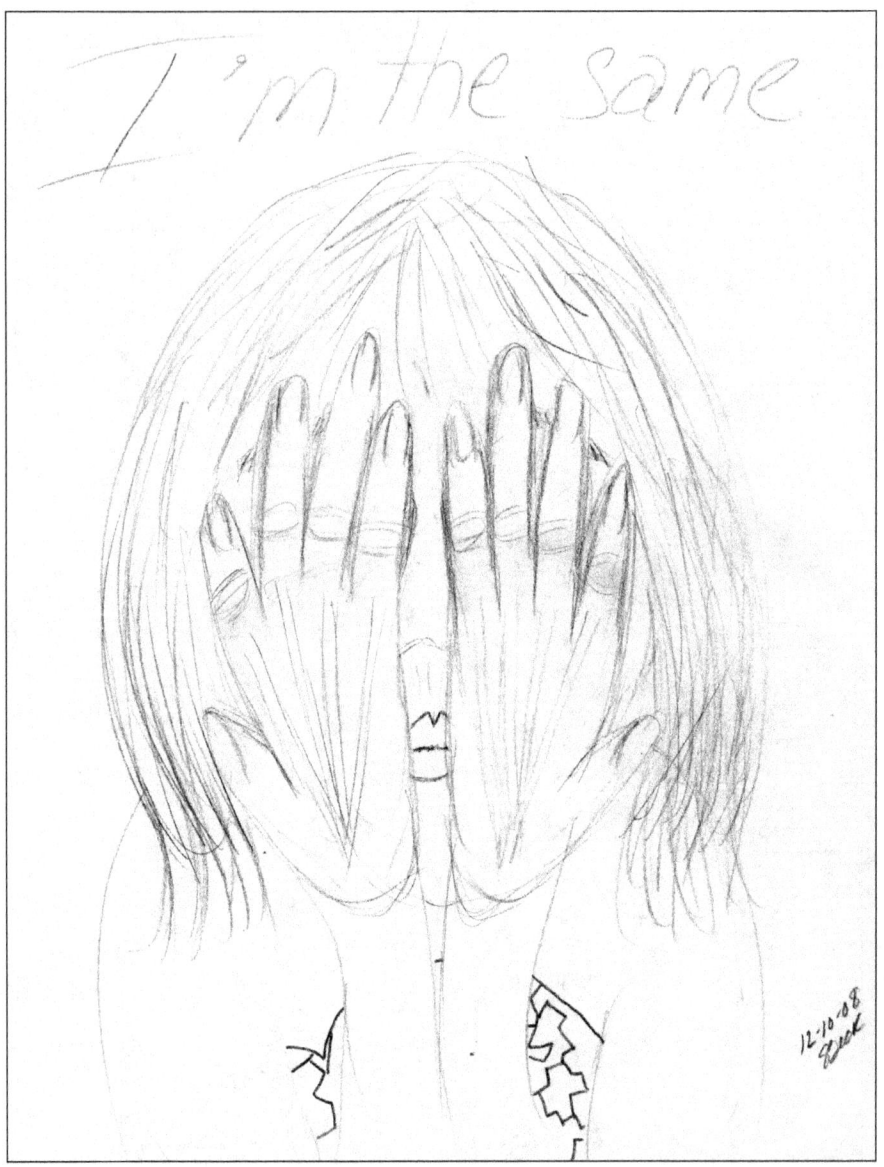

I'M THE SAME PERSON

That was me. I hid the shame and smiled to cover up
the darkness inside. We all wear masks of some kind.
Some are sheer, and some need to be opaque.

JOURNEY

I stayed in the same lane, drove the same routes, only to put the darkness on repeat. It was the easiest and most difficult road traveled.

LEARN HOW

I could be told a thousand times and would never believe it. "You are beautiful. I love you!" is a life-changing experience when you land in a place of self-acceptance.

TEN TWO TWENTY ELEVEN

This date, October 2, 2011, changed many lives. It was the day my daughters lost their father, my ex-mother-in-law lost her son, and many others lost a friend. I lost a person with whom I once adored and loved.

I CAN'T

I could not process the news of his death. My brain would not allow it to be real. I listened to the phone message left by my ex-mother-in-law, listened to it again, and froze.

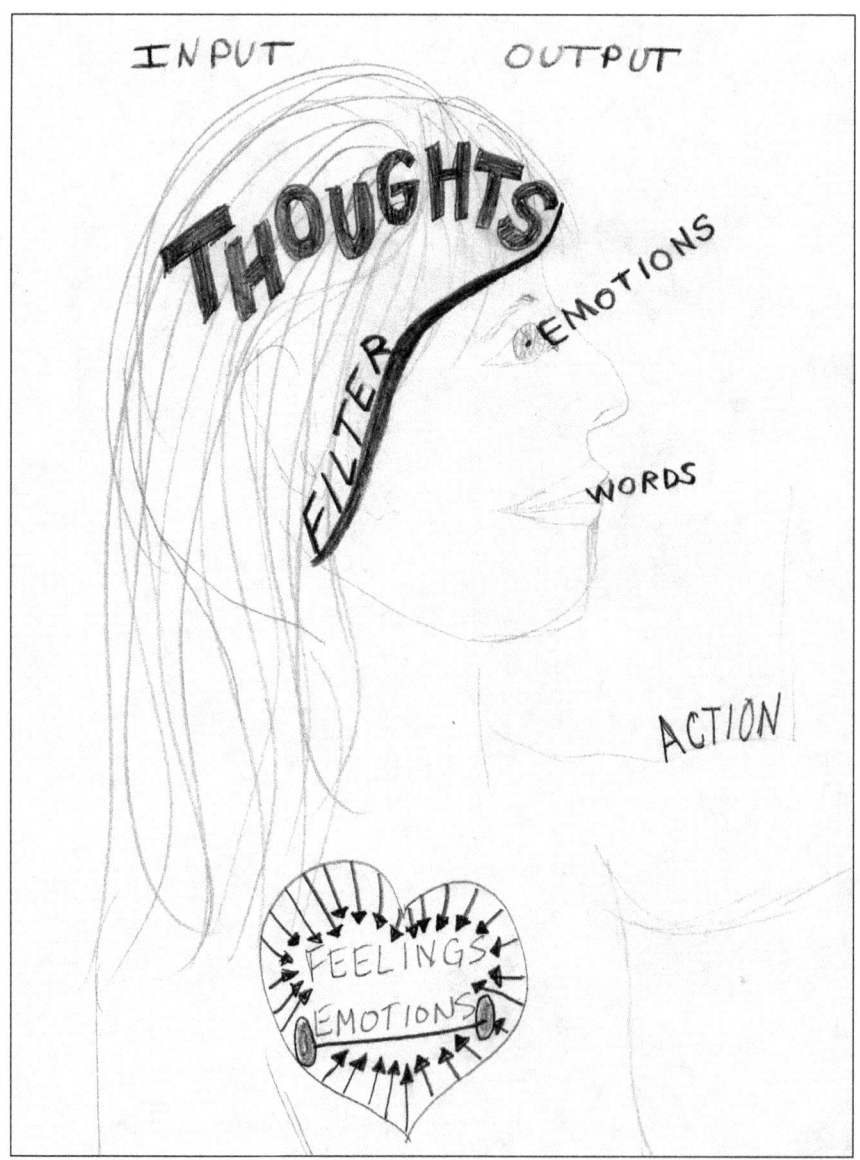

INPUT-OUTPUT

There are events in life that leave a person reeling. Understanding
them helps process feelings and emotions. Part of that process
is input and output. Give folks a chance to process.

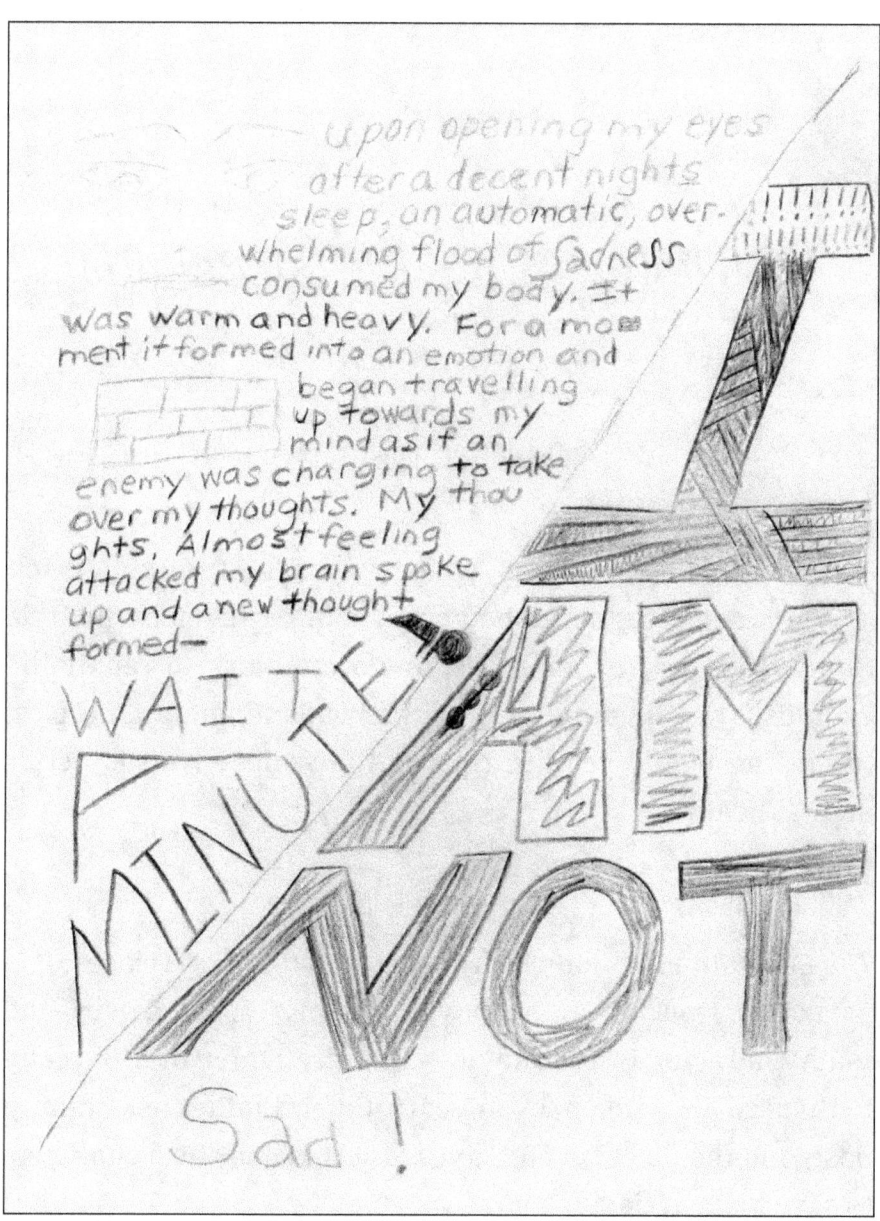

REALIZATION

My self-talk changed its tune to proclaim,
"Wait a minute! I am not sad!"

Backstories for the Drawings

BALANCE OF DECEPTION

W HEN THE STAKES WERE AT THEIR HIGHEST, I felt depleted; mind, body, and soul. My choices: hold on to my traumatic experiences, or do the work to repair the wounds. This dilemma was a crossroads moment. The path to healing would require tipping the scales towards better mental health.

DARE TO LOVE

The Love Dare is a book written to strengthen marriages. It is part of the storyline of the movie *Fireproof* (2008). Caleb —the main character in the movie— is a firefighter and is ready to divorce his wife of seven years. Caleb's father asks him to postpone the decision and gives him this book as a challenge to save his marriage.

My husband, Rob, is going on year 25 as a volunteer firefighter for our local county fire department, serving as Assistant Fire Chief for the latter part of those years. He planned a date for dinner and to see the movie *Fireproof*. I thought it would be like the movie *Backdraft*. The theater was packed, and the only seats available were in the front row next to the plant manager at Rob's work. Once I saw what the movie was about, I wanted to escape. It felt as if the audience was watching our private troubles on the screen.

We survived the date. The movie left an impression. Day 10 in the *Love Dare* book is: Love is Unconditional. The dare is to do something out of the ordinary for your spouse. Caleb chose to turn the coffee pot on each morning as a thoughtful gesture. Rob has done the same ever since watching this movie. It truly is the little things.

TRAPPED IN TEARS

I experienced vulnerability and insecurity at their finest. There were times when I would break down and cry for no reason at all and for all kinds of reasons. Since giving up my job to move to South Korea, I was dependent upon another. Vince had control of the finances; I wasn't on the checking account. It was the opposite with Rob, but I still could not shake that feeling of dependency. My mom was the sole provider, and perhaps I was insecure about not filling that role.

THE SELF

An introspective look at the self is no easy task. "Who R You?" I found myself trying to answer who I was and who I wanted to be. I felt so complex and gave my answer in four categories: Life, Love, Live, and Learn. This quest is going back to the basics so I can start to rebuild.

DEAR FAMILY

"I will listen, and your love will fill my heart." I had to be in charge and be the sole problem-solver, so I thought. I lived in alert mode. What I needed was to get out of my way.

A PEACE OF TIME

Time management or a juggling act? There is only so much time in a day a person can be productive and stay healthy. I was not conscious of this. My clock became crowded. As a homemaker, I was running on busy time - all - the - time. If I was to reach inner peace, I needed to learn to balance my time more appropriately.

COVERED IN PAIN

I have a difficult time reflecting on this drawing. I am married to a man who kept trying to show me a normal relationship, and instead of embracing him and his love, I kept the burden of my inner suffering all to myself—a selfish move on my part in the name of protecting my pain. The difficulty is in the regret that I didn't free myself of this pain sooner.

ANXIETY

I did not recognize my anxiety or depression. I had tired spells, retired early to bed, and took naps. My kids know I was present, but I was exhausted. I wore myself out physically, emotionally, and mentally. And then I crashed.

I'M NO EINSTEIN

My husband is a scientist; I am an emotional rollercoaster.

We look at most everything from these lenses. His $e = mc^2$ equation is different from mine. Where he saw energy, I desired emotion. I felt stuck in my inability to communicate and frustrated that I could not translate his. I was looking for a connection on an emotional level. With my skewed thoughts, I could not compute.

WHAT HAVE I DONE?

I did not realize that I wasn't the only one in pain. My daughter was experiencing her kind of pain. During my brief separation from her stepdad, she had been cutting. I had been so distracted by my own perceived loneliness and dissatisfaction in my marriage that I failed to see how it affected my children. She had been cutting. Shock, sadness, and guilt overpowered me when she did show me. This discovery happened when she told me about that psycho counselor and what he tried to do to her.

HAMLET

While in therapy, my daughters were on my mind; I wanted them back.

All spoke foul words, and there was no immediate resolution in sight. Repairing our relationship remained my focus even while working to fix myself.

My girls can tell you how dramatic I can be. I love theater. I dreamt of being on stage someday. Shakespeare's *Hamlet* inspired me to do this drawing. The novel was a reading assignment in a theater class I took in my early attempts at college. The Shakespearean language was just as foreign to me as knowing how to raise teenage girls. I had no clue until the professor translated Hamlet's 'To be, or not to be' soliloquy to the class. The slings and arrows of outrageous fortune came back to me when thinking about the status of my relationship with my daughters – "Ay, there's the rub."

IT'S NOT ABOUT ME

The most challenging part about therapy for me was the self-reflection. It was easier to share the stories about what other people had done to me than how I responded to them. Then, the therapist steps in and points out some new ways to look at things. Instead of focusing on what they did, the focus was on how to process my long-standing reactions.

After pouring out the pain of one story, my therapist looked directly at me and softly asked, "Is it still happening?" It took me a moment, and there was some resistance to let go of my story, then I responded, "No." I lived my present by holding on to my past and projecting them outward when I became triggered. The therapist's question and my answer permitted me to let go of stories no longer active. I began to heal for the first time since I was eight years old.

TOOLBOX 101

The road to inner peace was hard because I didn't know how to do it. The easy and quick fix was to sweep the crap into a DB and run away. I felt safe in the CBT setting, enabling me to consider new thoughts, alternative skills and develop strategies. For the first time, I began separating myself from each issue. This process launched the healing within.

Indeed, it is easier said than done when dealing with an emotional excavation. Digging deep requires tools, knowledge, and process. I had more risk than protective factors, leaving my toolbox scarce and damaged. To achieve peace, I needed continued access to and willingness to receive therapy.

TOOLBOX 102

I hid the detours on my life journey, so the roads I took appeared less rocky. A deeper look revealed I had been traveling on survival lane and suddenly ran out of gas. I built walls instead of caution signs and hogged the road at times. If someone got too close to my protective barrier, I became triggered. Often, I felt the need to defend myself based on the past and not the present circumstances. I would take the hypervigilance exit to stop the war within (Hypervigilance, 2021). My journey became more manageable once I learned that I could take a different road.

SOMETIMES

Not asking for help when you need it is a trauma response. I equated asking for help as a form of weakness. That feeling led to vulnerability, and I dreaded the exposure. Fixing my brokenness was not accomplished on my own, and the repair continues. I had to take possession of my stinkin' thinkin' and guide it in a different direction. The first step was to recognize that I needed help.

Typical trauma responses include fear response, loss of control, flashbacks, trouble concentrating, guilty feelings, negative self-image, depression, and disruptive relationships

(Victim Reactions to Traumatic Events Handout - National Crime Victims Research and Treatment Center, n.d.). If this were a list, I could checkmark each of those responses. I was never able or ready to pause long enough to seek help to overcome these issues. This fact calls for normalizing mental health and making access to care more attainable. Please repeat after me: Mental health care should be part of our routine health care.

NOT ALONE

"When the student is ready, the teacher will appear" is a quote shared with me in therapy that resonates with me deeply. There were nuggets of advice from loving friends and family, but I was not ready to listen; not listening can be isolating, and not listening led me to the point of feeling broken down and unsalvageable. Acknowledging this led me to be ready to do the work. The outside world did not feel safe to me. Inside therapy's safety, I could objectively receive insight from counselors and strangers going through their struggles. Participation in professional and mini discussions is vital.

Group therapy was a big part of my mental health recovery process. Individual troubles are unique, but we were all there for healing. Somehow, by sharing our despairs, we were able to speak up and help others. At the end of each day, and upon discharge, we went our separate ways. I will be forever grateful for the group therapy process and hopeful for successful journeys for anyone down that road to improve their mental health.

INJURIES

Comminuted fractures can break a bone into several pieces. Injuries to the mind and body can feel like fractures to the soul. Some heal better and faster than others. Some require help to get out of the darkness.

Hidden in a dark place of my soul were my adverse personal experiences. I believed I caused those wounds, so they were my responsibility alone. The physical bruises and aches resolve through homeostasis. It was the emotional residual that left the injuries clinging to my soul. Left unaddressed, I would take a road trip to darkness. That's how it was for me, internally.

I'M FINE!

Well, hot dang! That's a confused mind, a complex soul. It is shocking that I locked and loaded those memories in my DB for so long. I didn't want anyone to know that part of me. I still shudder inside when I revisit this drawing. My breath is sucked away, my eyes swell, and my mind goes into "Claire Fraser" overdrive – Jesus H Roosevelt Christ! (a nod to the book *Outlander* by Diana Gabaldon). I take a controlling breath in and slowly exhale. Then say to me, "It's not happening anymore."

I'M THE SAME PERSON

Sometimes I was the one quietly sitting in the corner; other times, I was voicing my opinion. Okay, more so of the latter. When my words did not match the circumstance, my husband says he would wonder what was going on with me, not in a way to make fun but to seek understanding. He saw me suffocating in pain but didn't know what had happened to me. He didn't make me feel like something was "wrong" with me. This distinction was made clear after reading *What Happened to You?* by Bruce D. Perry, MD, Ph.D., and Oprah Winfrey.

I was trying to hide what had happened to me because I didn't want people to know what was wrong with me. There were times when I was unsuccessful. I was at work one of those times, and a co-worker caught me in the bathroom stall crying uncontrollably. Instead of the bladder erupting, it was my soul crashing. I was going through a divorce with kids this time and felt hopeless and lost.

This episode reminds us to be kind to others as we never know the suffering they are carrying. Be grateful for the heroes who show up to catch you when you fall. That day in the bathroom, a woman whose name means beautiful in Spanish checked in on me, comforted me, and gave me her shoulder to cry on. She showed me that not all people mean to harm you. This memory is tear-producing to me to this day.

JOURNEY

"Life is a journey, not a destination." – Ralph Waldo Emerson. It was easy going down the same road. That was all I knew. It was like taking a 1,591-mile road trip with no bathroom breaks or fuel refills. The engine was bound to blow up, and accidents would happen. Like a car, a person needs routine maintenance. Not addressing my traumas prevented me from reaching a peaceful destination, let alone enjoying the journey.

I am grateful to be traveling with a lighter emotional load. I stop and refuel when my cup feels empty, and I take breaks when I am overwhelmed. I look at life differently than before. Taking a more organic approach to life has allowed me to live free. There is still pending work on the emotional detachment road, but I enjoy the journey.

LEARN HOW

There are times when I see the outer beauty in the mirror and times when I see a reflection of an empty soul. After outpatient therapy, continued counseling, and a bit of time passing, I began to see my worth for who I was and what I had accomplished. The internal view was the most important.

Every day, my husband, Rob, tells me he loves me. When I doubted my self-love, I also questioned his love for me. With a clear heart and mind, I appreciate his expression of love, and now I believe him.

TEN TWO TWENTY ELEVEN

I had opened a small fitness studio teaching yoga and Zumba classes. Not long after starting, we got the news about the death of my ex-husband. I went into crisis mode to help my girls walk through this tragedy. They were 17 and 19.

My eldest daughter was at college, four hours away. What words would sufficiently give her the information and at the same time does not cause her pain? It was urgent news, and there was an urgency in contacting her before word got out, and she was made aware by the talk of the town.

My other daughter was home and already in a vulnerable state over her relationship with her dad. This misfortune could destroy her; it did in many ways.

It wasn't until January of 2012 that I realized I had become depressed again and had been pulling my hair out. Trichotillomania. I self-referred to outpatient therapy once again. There I processed my shock and emotions about the death of my ex-husband.

I CAN'T

It was a Sunday afternoon; Graciela played outdoors with a neighbor's niece, Rob was at a fire call, and Victoria and I were chilling at home.

I checked my phone and saw that I had a message. I couldn't understand the message correctly. I didn't even move into crisis mode immediately. I stepped outside and called my neighbor and asked her if Graciela could stay with her for a while. I explained that I got a message that said my daughter's father was dead and that I would take Victoria in town to her aunt's house to see what was going on.

Still, I could not come up with any words. I told Victoria that her Meme had called, and something was going on, that we needed to go to Aunt Linda's house. I drove, and my usual talkative self could not come up with any words to tell my daughter that her dad was found dead in his room while at work on a riverboat.

We got to Aunt Linda's house and walked in. I told Meme that I couldn't tell her. So, she did. And that's when Victoria fell straight down to the ground and cried out, "Nooooooooooooo!"

INPUT-OUTPUT

The loss of my ex-husband so struck me. Although I did not think it was my loss to grieve, I could not understand why it caused extraordinary sadness and depressed feelings. We were divorced, not on friendly terms or in a good place when this happened. I also felt that I had nowhere and no right to grieve or someone to share my grieving with.

The knowledge that my daughters lost their father also left me with the feeling of more parental responsibility than I could handle. I had to work hard to understand that they would need to work through this loss their way and that I would be there in a supporting role as a parent. This time allowed me to let go of many controls I had placed on my husband, Rob, and let him be a part of that support.

REALIZATION

Self-talk can push your emotions around as a school bully tries to over-power others with words and actions. It can work the opposite and be your best friend when you need to pump up. One day, long after both admissions in outpatient therapy, I came to a new realization.

"Upon opening my eyes after a decent night's sleep, an automatic, overwhelming flood of sadness consumed my body. It was warm and heavy. For a moment, it formed into emotion and began traveling up towards my mind as if an enemy was charging to take over my thoughts—my thoughts. Almost feeling attacked, my brain spoke up, and a new thought formed. *Wait a minute! I am not sad!*"

PART V

Healed-Soul

THESE CHAPTERS ARE RECOLLECTIONS of my experience post-CBT. They recount steps taken towards continued healing that reshaped my views of marriage, relationships, and me.

I MADE IT OUT OF THE DARKNESS, but it still required management and self-checks to keep from returning there. I credit going to therapy for preparing me to cope with future difficulties. I can shut down at times and rise to the occasion other times.Raising children could have been a better experience, but it could have been worse. For the most part, we had a great life. It's those darn detours that get you! I could have been a better mother and wife, but I could have been worse. A husband treating me, his wife, the right way despite my flaws, fears, and the DB I carried was a blessing.

WHAT MATTERS IS THAT WE ARE ALIVE AND WELL.

Discharge Plan

MY DISCHARGE PLAN INCLUDED MEDICATION and continued appointments with a counselor. I would travel about 45 minutes to attend a counseling session and see the psychiatrist for medication management. I slowly worked through the residual conflicts, memories, and emotions that contributed to my depression and anxiety. This allowed me to start healing my family; in a healthy manner and with a healthier me.

Over time, the progress I had made in understanding past traumas and how to manage present conflicts with my daughters and my husband outweighed the need for medication. The Lexapro left me feeling more zombie-like, and I did not want that. I needed medication while going through an acute episode of major depressive disorder (MDD). The counseling sessions left me with a feeling of self-awareness and understanding. I also picked up a few more life tools in my toolbox. Sometimes I forget they are there; I don't even realize I have used them.

Dealing with the Past Now

WHERE DID SHE GO?

THANKFULLY, MY MOM IS STILL WITH US AS of the writing of this book. When I think about her, I understand she has a story that is not unlike my own and is deserving of grace. We are continuously gardening our adult relationship. She has her emotional capacity, and I have mine. We listen to each other in love.

SIBLING RIVALRY

My sisters and I have unique adult relationships. I communicate with Joanne when I must but stay out of her radar; I no longer have to be her target. The only regret with this strategy is that it has put some distance between me and her children and grandchildren.

My sister, Gigi, remains one of my best friends, confidants, and yes, she is and will always be 'Mother Gigi.' This relationship can be good and bad at times, but we have a bond together and always work through any challenges.

As for my little brother, Roman, he now lives with me and my husband, Rob, in Illinois. My mother made the difficult decision to transfer his legal guardianship to me in 2018, even if it meant moving him across the country to avoid going into a group home. She lives in an assisted living apartment setting and lives her best life surrounded by others, and seems to be a busy lady.

I DON'T LIKE PILLS

I went into surgery to have a cyst on my ovary removed. When I woke up, I learned doctors had to remove the ovary and other reproductive organs—they did a complete hysterectomy.

I had already been taking Lexapro to help my depression and anxiety, and now I was taking two pills. I worked hard to get to a place where I did not need the Lexapro, and after many years on the Estradiol, I stopped taking that pill.

Now I must watch out for my cholesterol, or I will need to start on a statin pill. I don't want to take any pills because it still reminds me of that one time long ago. There may come a time when I will need to overcome this trigger and take the necessary medication to support a healthy life.

RUNAWAY

As far as running away, physically, I find it tempting to do so to be back home with my family. After raising my kids, it's a challenging situation since that was the initial reason for staying in Illinois. To my husband's credit, he did start the ball rolling to get us there in our retirement years. Concerning people, I recommend 'walking' in any form—walk for health reasons and walk away from unhealthy relationships.

NEIGHBORLY

It took about 33 years, but my mom finally sold her house and moved away from the neighborhood we grew up in since I was in 7th grade. I dealt with anxiety each time I drove up to her home, even when that couple had moved away. I don't have to see it anymore and remember the awful time and the vile man who took advantage of a vulnerable 16-year-old.

BIRTH CERTIFICATE GUY

I am not alone in not having a dad around to teach me things that dads teach their daughters. That time has passed. The bitterness and disgust towards my biological father stayed with me for years. I was in South Korea when I learned that he had succumbed to Lou Gehrig's disease. I thought that the memories of his attempt to have sex with me would die with him, but they did not. It was still in the DB.

In late 2021 I had a conversation with my mom about this. I questioned if he was my "real" dad, and she assured me that he was. She also reinforced the fact that he was an evil man. This certainty, albeit late, was what I needed for a final resolution on this subject.

MY FIRST I DO

It's not that I didn't care about Steve. I believed I would be married for life when I said "I do;" it was in a church, for goodness sake. After the divorce, we both moved on, and I haven't seen him in over 30 years. I can only wish he is well wherever he is.

MY CHOICE

When I must fill out medical information forms, the miscarriage I had comes to mind since I have to write that I had been pregnant four times and have had three live births. That information will always be a part of me.

MY SECOND I DO

Since deciding to leave the country and marry into the military, I have been on some adventures. I could never regret making this choice as it produced my two precious older daughters. If we did anything right, we did this. I'll never have the chance to address my personal experiences with him since he left this world at 43. I do my best to share memories here and there with my older girls so they remember him and know that he loved them very much. If there is any consolation for me, it was when my middle daughter shared with me that sometimes they would talk about me and that he did love me.

DIVORCE 2.0

I've been divorced twice! I tried for the third time, but my husband did not have it. Being divorced with no kids is one thing but going through a bitter divorce with very young children is another matter. If you're unfortunate to have to go through the latter, please keep the peace for your children's sake, don't talk bad about the other parent. In time they will make an impression on both of you as parents, and you never know if they will ever get to see them again.

NOW WHAT

I meant what I said when I said, "I do." Sometimes things change, and as REO Speedwagon sings, you've got to roll with the changes. As Chumbawamba sings, I get knocked down, but I get up again, and this world will never keep me down. Music is very healing.

THE LAST I DO

I made a fair assessment of Rob when I accepted his marriage proposal. I didn't know what he saw in me, but I decided that if I were to live my life raising my girls in this funky ole town, I would want to do it with someone I could trust with my heart around my girls. We did and are doing the best we can with our circumstances. I will be forever grateful to my pastor for his advice to not take the action of a divorce right away and to my husband for giving me just enough rope to hang myself and being there to cut it down and catch me. He gave me the space I needed to walk through the steps that CBT would take me and was there when I came out a healthier mother, wife, and human being. I still get on his nerves, and he on mine, but we are more connected. As husband and wife, we have grown individually, and we have made it 23 years as of May 2022.

Discovery

MY DEAR HUSBAND

WE CELEBRATED OUR 22nd WEDDING ANNIVERSARY in May 2021. Our communication has improved, and I sometimes wish he would stop interrupting my thinking. But we laugh, we walk, we share, and we love.

While searching for support documentation for some of the topics I have shared in this book, I came across an article on Emotional Detachment *(Emotional Detachment: What It Is and How to Overcome It, 2019)*. I immediately jumped on the link to read to have a "see what I mean" moment. I begged Rob for years to communicate with me and could not understand why he would shut me out of his thoughts. As I read the symptoms of emotional detachment, I began to see that those symptoms described me! Was I the one emotionally detached? Mouth open wide moment. I had to let this sink in.

I sat down with my husband and asked to talk with him, not start a fight, only share. I let him know of my discovery. I declared that I was asking him for something I was unwilling to give myself. This realization was revealing for both of us. It was heartfelt and eye-opening.

Another discovery I made was in the tone and volume of his voice. If Rob's everyday voice was calm and his volume was at level one, Vince's regular voice was an excited level eight and went to a level 10 plus when he became angry. Rob maintained calmness at the beginning of our courtship and marriage, and I felt safe and appreciated the predictability. Over time, I took this to mean he was unexcited and lacked emotion, which left me lonely or bored. That was a misinterpretation of his calm demeanor. I was missing the chaos because that is what I was used to. It didn't feel normal to live with calm. I accept and appreciate that calmness now.

Among many positive and other loving attributes I have learned to receive from Rob is that of his presence. He was always there, and I kept waiting for him to fail me, yell at me, come at me, and be like the other men who broke their promises. That wasn't Rob at all.

MY ADULT CHILDREN

The transition from raising my children to having a relationship with them as adults was different for them and me. I knew they would leave this town and most likely not return. That was a hard pill for me to swallow.

Vanessa was the eldest and went off to college; that was easy. We were supportive and proud of her goal-oriented mindset. She worked hard in high school and knew that college was in her future. She was able to attend a top university in Illinois and benefited from her dad's military service with a tuition waiver program. She earned her degree as a chemist and is working in her career field in Chicago. I do my best to tell her I am proud of her. She led the way towards her goals, and we played a supportive role. It is her world, and we are living in it.

Victoria, the middle child, is a survivor. We talk as much as possible, but she is busy with her twin daughters. She is married and lives in Las Vegas, Nevada. I'm a bit jealous of her living closer to my home state of Arizona and my family than I am. She has a story of her own that only she can tell. Our mother-daughter relationship has been tried many times, and I am grateful to say it has survived. Many costs came along the road to where we are today. We've talked about writing a book together and sharing our dual perspectives of the walks we have taken with each other. While we broke at times, we never gave up.

Graciela is the youngest and has seen her share of adverse childhood experiences (ACEs). These ACEs have affected some of her relationships with others, starting in middle school through high school. She was in the graduating class of 2020 and among the many high school students who did not have a regular final year because of the COVID-19 pandemic. She was a discus and shot-put thrower, and I coached her in high school. We did not get to participate in our final season. She attends a college in Chicago, hoping that she will get a glimpse of the actual college experience before graduating. Her first year in college was 100 percent online, and her sophomore year had a rough start. She remains a quiet soul and is very private. So, when she has time to talk, I listen. I let her know that I am here for her; even if I don't have all the answers, I have insight from a much healthier life perspective.

MY MOTHER

My dear sweet mother. God loves her. Until she finishes writing her memoirs, I have no idea what she had in her DB. I can only rely on my perception of how her life was, but it is skewed from my adolescent, young adult, and middle-aged lenses.

As a teen, I wanted to run away from her, made choices that left me far away from her, and sometimes scolded her for some choices she made later in life. But we know how to forgive each other.

A few crises arose over the past several years that had me flying to and from Arizona on an emergency level. The first time I left for two weeks and stayed another week, leaving my youngest daughter with her dad and relying on neighbors to get her to and from school. Subsequent visits were a mix of planned and emergent. I had always lived in fear when the phone rang, and it was someone from Arizona. Instead of "hello," it was "what's wrong?"

However, the past few years have been stable and a bit enriching. When I visit, I get to help my mom out with some things and enjoy our time together. We share insights that lead me to believe we may have similar experiences that damaged our psych and can relate to one another. I am on a journey to love myself where I am at and doing my best to love her where she is at. It does not matter if I am in my 50s and she is in her 80s. When I bring her mini diet coke cans, the joy she expresses is priceless!

MY SISTER

I got my sister, Gigi, on speed dial. I try to keep her in the loop, and she tries to do the same. We are both proud of how we have managed to survive our childhood and marriages and that we are still here standing. She has always worked full-time and has a different amount of free time than I do. I've got my brother with me, and she does what she can to help our mother. Sometimes I get a call to help her out with our mom (doctor's appointments and such), but mostly our calls are to get updates or ask me, "when are you coming back to Arizona." If she has a tired tone, I immediately go into "what happened" mode.

For most of my life, she has been the one to give me a shoulder to cry on, scold me when I needed it, and keep me updated on our family happenings back home. Our lives seemed to have balanced out, and now I feel that we can be there for each other or that I can be a shoulder for her if necessary.

MY BEST FRIEND

Cell phones are great. Neither of us needs to worry about the costs of long-distance telephone calls to catch up. Now, we are on pace and text recipes we've made, call to check-in, and rely on each other for support on the most minimal and excitable things. My friend has been as constant a friend as Rob has been a husband. We met in seventh grade, and she is the most extended friendship I have besides my sister and a couple of other lifelong friends.

She, of all people, would be the one I would turn to when life got tough. I didn't call her as often when I was in Georgia and Illinois because I was ashamed of the consequences of my decisions. I talked to her during my difficulties with Rob, and she remained nonjudgmental and supportive of me where I was at in life. She would send me cards of hope throughout the years and was one of the people I would make sure to see each time I visited Arizona.

She remains my bestie, my sister in heart, and my vault.

MY HOME

I realize I have nothing to complain about when it comes to having the necessities in life. I have always had a roof over my head, food to eat, clothes to wear; my children had the same. Sometimes we had help, and other times we were able to help others. We've been able to give our daughters extras in life and taught them the value of work. My husband has been working since he was 14 years old.

Our lovely home in a nice neighborhood is a blessing, and I have always felt safe, unlike the house and neighborhood where I grew up in. My husband made efforts to bring a little bit of Arizona into our home by embracing a Southwest theme and purchasing on eBay prints by DeGrazia, an artist from Tucson, Arizona, known for his colorful images of Native American children of the American Southwest and other Western scenes. (DeGrazia Gallery in the Sun Museum, 2021).

My time with my family has increased over the past three years. We invested in a home there and now have an Arizona address. We are thinking ahead to retirement and have a place to stay until we can make that home our primary home. Closer and closer, but I must still dig deep for patience.

Conclusion

I SET OUT TO WRITE A BOOK OF MY EXPERIENCES with the understanding that they are told only from my perspective. It's possible to get a different account from the individuals who have made it into my writings. We all have our unique lenses and processors. When the book *What Happened to You?: Conversations on Trauma, Resilience, and Healing,* by Bruce D. Perry, M.D., Ph.D., and Oprah Winfrey came out, I listened to it on Audible and then bought and read the hardback. It got me thinking, "hell yeah, I got a story to tell!" This book is my answer to their question. This book is about what happened to me.

During the writing process, I let my mother know I was writing a book and shared the challenges I was experiencing with her. She was also in the process of writing her memoirs. We both agreed that it was a gut-wrenching process. Both questioned if these events in our lives happened. We were there, we had these experiences, but they were so incredible to be true, even in our recollections. We both had to take breaks in our writing; in fact, she began the writing process before I started mine. I tried to encourage her and told her she should do this and how wonderful it would be to know more about her and how it was for her growing up. She was having challenges too. She called it writer's block, and I called it reliving the experience again but in color and with the emotional pain that matched the memories. I wasn't affected mentally, but the physical response to revisiting what happened to me had me feeling, metaphorically, the punches. She understood all too well what it meant to go back in time and visit the events and experiences that significantly impacted her life. It won't be easy for her, as it was not easy for me. I was able to share with her how therapeutic it was to get these experiences out, put them in writing with the knowledge that it is from our very own perspectives, and then leave them in a space that would make up chapters of our books. It can be very healing.

There are still days when I feel the weight of stress and sense the feeling of depression creeping. It usually hits in the morning when I wake. I handle it by using positive self-talk: Get up, get dressed, and open the curtains. I am also more open with my husband and talk through my thoughts, easing the burden of feeling that I am walking alone in this life.

My story is unique to me. But there are many others who have stories of struggles, challenges, and trauma that made it into their Dung Bag and have not had the opportunity to go through intensive CBT. That makes me sad. At the risk of exposure to my deepest emotions, if you have a Dung Bag of your own and you feel ready to dump it, I hope my stories give you the courage to seek a mental health assessment, CBT, counseling, or at least talk with someone you trust. The goal is to properly process and adequately place those traumatic memories in their rightful places. As Dr. Perry and Oprah Winfrey have suggested, it may be better not to focus on what is wrong with you but on what happened to you. The contents of your Dung Bag don't have to define you, and you don't have to forever carry it with you. You can get help through and out of the darkness. Make the journey yourself; you are worth it.

Bibliography

(n.d.). Retrieved from Land of Lincoln Legal Aid: https://lincolnlegal.org/

(n.d.). Retrieved from https://www.pxu.org/abril

About DSM-5. (n.d.). Retrieved from American Psychiatric Association: https://www.psychiatry.org/psychiatrists/practice/dsm

An analysis of out-of-wedlock births in the United States (1996, August 1). Retrieved from Brookings: https://www.brookings.edu/research/an-analysis-of-out-of-wedlock-births-in-the-united-states/

Beta Sigma Phi International (n.d.). Retrieved from http://www.betasigmaphi.org/login.php?ret_link=%2FSurvey%2Fsurvey_entry_multi.php&type=notLogged

Bostrom Alternative Center (n.d.). Retrieved from Phoenix Union High School District: https://www.pxu.org/bostrom

Boyles, S. (2005, January 12). Depression Risk Worsens Through Generations. Retrieved from www.webmd.com: https://www.webmd.com/depression/news/20050112/depression-risk-worsens-through-generations

DeGrazia Gallery in the Sun Museum (2021). Retrieved from https://degrazia.org/about-degrazia/bio/

Emotional Detachment: What It Is and How to Overcome It. (2019, September 3). Retrieved from Healthline: https://www.healthline.com/health/mental-health/emotional-detachment#symptoms

Hypervigilance (2021, September 24). Retrieved from Wikipedia: https://en.wikipedia.org/wiki/Hypervigilance

Lott, T. (2013, April 20). Tim Lott's Family Column. Retrieved from *The Guardian*: Love may be important, but communication, respect and trust are essential: https://www.theguardian.com/lifeandstyle/2013/apr/20/love-not-all-need-marriage

Miscarriage (2017, November). Retrieved from March of Dimes: https://www.marchofdimes.org/complications/miscarriage.aspx

National Crime Victims Research and Treatment Center, M. U. (n.d.). Victim Reactions to Traumatic Events Handout. Retrieved from https://www.dartmouth.edu/eap/reactionstotrauma.pdf#:~:text=Depression%3A%20Another%20common%20reaction%20to%20trauma%20is%20a,previously%20enjoyable%20often%20accompanies%20these%20feelings%20of%20sadness.

Tracy, N. (2015, February 13). Teen Suicide Rates Statistics and Facts. Retrieved from Healthy Place: https://www.healthyplace.com/suicide/teen-suicide-rates-statistics-and-facts

Welner, D. M. (2010, October 18). Child Sexual Abuse, 6 Stages of Grooming. Retrieved from www.Oprah.com: https://www.oprah.com/oprahshow/child-sexual-abuse-6-stages-of-grooming/all

What is Down Syndrome? (2021, April 6). Retrieved from Center for Disease Control and Prevention: https://www.cdc.gov/ncbddd/birthdefects/downsyndrome.html

When Will My Child Stop Bedwetting? (2021, March 26). Retrieved from Good Nites: https://www.goodnites.com/en-us/bedwetting/what-is-bedwetting/when-will-my-child-stop-bedwetting

Wikimedia Commons (2021, February 20). Retrieved from https://commons.wikimedia.org/wiki/File:Phoenix,_AZ,_El_Norteno_%22Dios_Bendiga_Este_Negocio%22_-_God_Bless_This_Business_-_Joanne_Kennedy_Ramos,_Artist,_2011._Beloved_Osbaldo_Andrews_Bedoy,_11-23-95_to_03-06-03_%22May_our_Young_Mariachi_Watch_Over_Us_With_th_-_panoramio.jpg

Wikipedia. (2021, June 4). Retrieved from Sibling Rivalry: https://en.wikipedia.org/wiki/Sibling_rivalry#cite_note-:0-2

Wikipedia. (2021, July 5). National Suicide Prevention Lifeline. Retrieved from Wikipedia, The Free Encyclopedia: https://en.wikipedia.org/wiki/National_Suicide_Prevention_Lifeline

Wikipedia. (2021, July 4). Statutory Rape. Retrieved from Wikipedia, the Free Encyclopedia: https://en.wikipedia.org/wiki/Statutory_rape

About the Author

*S*ABRINA BECK has been on the run emotionally since she was 16 years old. The *Dung Bag Road* is her first published book, and it is fitting that she should write about how she benefited from cognitive-behavioral therapy (CBT) in the hopes of helping others. She has been called many things, but author and artist had never made it onto that list until now.

Sabrina has been a resident of Illinois since 1994. She received a Bachelor of Science degree in Workforce, Education, and Development in 2003, and an Applied Science degree in Health Information Technology in 2016. For many years, she has been a housewife, holds a substitute teacher certification, is a volunteer track throws coach for the local high school, and is currently a caregiver for her brother.

She is Mom to three daughters, Nana of twin granddaughters, and a wife to Rob for over 22 years. She has served in officer roles for Zeta Zeta Sorority and has been a member since 1996. In 2014, she received the Massac County Helping Hands Award from United Way-Metropolis. Sabrina was a Massac County Drug Awareness Coalition (MCDAC) member from

2012 to 2020 and served on the Executive Board for many years. She was an integral part of the Drug-Free Communities Support Program federal grant committee, which was awarded to MCDAC in 2020.

Sabrina reads and listens to books for fun and therapeutic benefits, practices sewing, enjoys walking, and participates in Senior Olympics. In January 2008, she fulfilled a dream of being on stage by playing a lead role in *The Underpants* at the Market House Theater in Paducah, Kentucky. She has participated in the Senior Olympics and finished fourth place in both discus and shot put at the 2019 National Senior Games in Albuquerque, New Mexico.

Her story is filled with rough little edges, but she is courageous and committed to better mental health for herself and her children. She has overcome many obstacles in life, reaching a point in her journey battling depression where it is safe to share her story. She hopes to help others along their healing journey.

www.ingramcontent.com/pod-product-compliance
Lightning Source LLC
Chambersburg PA
CBHW061148120626
46546CB00005B/1975